Contemplative by Design

Contemplative by Design

Creating Quiet Spaces for Retreats, Workshops, Churches, and Personal Settings

Gerrie L. Grimsley and Jane J. Young

UPPER ROOM BOOKS®
NASHVILLE

Page 108 constitutes a continuation of the copyright page.

LIBRARY OF CONGRESS CATALOGING-IN-PUBLICATION DATA

Grimsley, Gerrie L.
  Contemplative by design : creating quiet spaces for retreats, workshops,
churches, and personal settings / Gerrie L. Grimsley and Jane J. Young.
    p. cm.
  Includes bibliographical references and index.
  ISBN 978-0-8358-9969-7 (alk. paper)
  1. Contemplation. 2. Meditation. 3. Quietism. 4. Sacred space.
I. Young, Jane J. II. Title.
  BV5091.C7G75 2008   263'.042—dc22   2008015803

Printed in the United States of America

Contents

Acknowledgments

We are deeply grateful to Sharon Conley, Kathleen Stephens, and Jeannie Crawford-Lee of The Upper Room. Sharon introduced the two of us and invited us to work together in 2006. Kathleen saw the possibilities of sharing the quiet space designs developed that summer and supported and guided the coordination that goes into writing even a small book. Finally, Jeannie's editorial work polished the text.

Many thanks go to Mary Lou Redding, Sophia Woods, Mike Smith, and Darlene Johnson, who read and responded to a draft manuscript, and to Betsy Hardin, who responded to Jane's poetry. Their insights, questions, and suggestions were immeasurably helpful.

We also extend appreciation to Sylvia Everett for permission to use a photograph of her art, to Laurette Wolfe for the family tree design, and to Martha Morrison and Marianne Borg for recommending books for further reading.

We offer thanks for the ideas, prayers, support, and inspiration of Marjorie J. Thompson, John Mogabgab, Flora Slosson Wuellner, Melissa Tidwell, Cheryl Jackson, Debbie White, Joan Floyd, Kate Rudd, Jud Hayes, Jean Cassidy, and Theresa Leatherwood.

And finally, sincere gratitude goes to our patient, helpful, and supportive husbands, Greg and Garland, who forgave our months-long affairs with computers and welcomed us back.

Preface

We did not yet know each other when we were invited by Upper Room Ministries to plan quiet spaces for their 2006 SOULfeast conference. From our first interaction, however, it was clear that both of us—Gerrie, an Upper Room staff member from Nashville, Tennessee, and Jane, a resident of Lake Junaluska, North Carolina, where the conference was to be held—considered ourselves called to the ministry of developing quiet spaces. After months of planning via e-mail and phone, we met for the first time the day before SOULfeast began.

Plans, work, and prayer for the quiet spaces brought us joy, but one of the greatest blessings was seeing how the fruits of our labor of love affected many SOULfeast participants. We had designed each quiet space as an invitation to conference goers and staff to withdraw from their busy schedules for sabbath rest. As we read and listened to evaluations of this five-day spiritual formation conference, expressions of gratitude for the quiet spaces assured us of the value of, and the need for, these areas.

Through both verbal and written communication, church leaders said they wanted—or were already making plans—to take what they had seen and experienced through these quiet spaces back to their churches or small groups. Because of their comments and requests for details and guidance, this book was born.

We wish you blessings as you develop and offer quiet spaces to all who come your way.

Prayerfully,
Gerrie Grimsley and Jane Young

Introduction

We yearn for rest, and our souls hunger to be fed, yet we seldom give ourselves permission to respond to these yearnings. The quiet spaces described in these pages are places intentionally designed to invite sabbath rest and to encourage reflection on, and quiet awareness of, the Spirit of God. Many of the spaces incorporate a visual focus, and all contain a simple, written meditation guide based on the premise that we are immersed in the sacred and can become more sensitive to that reality.

In this book you will find guidance and resources to develop such quiet spaces within a church, home, garden, conference, camp, or retreat setting. Quiet spaces may also be appropriate in centers of work or communal living such as hospitals, colleges, and retirement villages. Fifteen chapters present fifteen quiet space plans, and each chapter consists of three parts. First, an overview gives the theological, historical, or philosophical foundation for the particular quiet space.

Next, there are detailed instructions for its physical preparation. Then, a Participant's Guide to the quiet space is provided. The instructions and the guide may be used as written, simplified, supplemented, adapted in any way, or simply read to activate your own creativity. The chapter "General Considerations" offers recommendations applicable to all quiet spaces.

You need no special expertise to follow the suggestions in this book or to create other meaningful quiet spaces. The only requirements are a prayerful heart and willing hands. If you commit to this task, however, you are likely to experience both the satisfaction of meaningful effort and a deepened awareness of the holiness of all creation.

A person's experience within a quiet space will naturally be affected by his or her own needs and receptivity, but the space itself and the available written guide will offer the seeker a gentle hand on the path to awareness of the sacred.

Contemplative silence can lead to depths where longings are revealed and the presence of the One for whom we long is known.

How can it be that we can say
our God is everywhere
yet hours pass, and we do not sing
a single Alleluia?

Could it be that a minute shift
of focus, of attention,
will unveil a feast of the sacred
within our every day?

A carefully designed quiet space will say, *Discover the feast. Taste. Be fed.*

—ᘜ—

A Prayer to Consider Making Your Own

Give me a candle of the Spirit, O God, as I go down into the deep of my own being.
Show me the hidden things. Take me down to the spring of my life, and tell me my nature and name.
Give me freedom to grow so that I may become the self, the seed of which thou didst plant in me
at my making. Out of the deep I cry unto thee, O Lord.[1]
—George Appleton

CHAPTER 1

All of Life

If I take the wings of the morning
and settle at the farthest limits of the sea,
even there your hand shall lead me,
and your right hand shall hold me fast.
—Psalm 139:9-10

—⁓—

All beauties and wonders, all bright, blue skies,
All honest reflections or questions, "Why?"
Can lead to a sense of the presence of God.

But even mid terror, God's near as our breath.
In all we can whisper, in life or in death,
"Now into your hands, I commit my spirit."

Overview

Faith tells us that even when we do not see the evidence, God is actively involved in all of life. At the moment of birth, in the playfulness of a child, in the questions of a teenager, in the monotony of daily chores, in the loss of a loved one, in concern for an ill pet—God is there. In the excitement of new friendship, in the pain of an ended relationship, in the eagerness of a goal almost reached, in the disappointment of a dream unrealized, in the beauty of a sunset, in the devastation of war, in the silent cry of the abused, in the shame of the abuser, in the emptiness of a lost soul, in the peaceful joy of growing in Christ—in all things God hears, God sees, God is aware. This fundamental truth is taught in the earliest years of Sunday school, preached from the pulpit weekly, and often reiterated at the lowering of a casket.

We easily recognize God's involvement when prayers are answered to our satisfaction or when life goes well and hope abounds. We don't easily remember that God is still involved when life is disappointing, painful, or cruel, or when boredom sets in and life seems to move in slow motion. In unpleasant situations we sometimes question, *Where is God? Why doesn't God do something?*

On Wednesday nights, a pastor invites the congregation to remember and describe any "God sightings" from the week. Each person is encouraged to share details of when, where, and how she or he saw or experienced God's involvement either personally or in the life of someone else. A few raise hands almost immediately, while others struggle to think of a time they saw God at work.

It takes conscious effort and discipline to look for and recognize God in all of life. Yet to do so can bring about a stronger faith, greater awareness of the person of God who cares dearly for all of creation. We can get a clearer glimpse of the incomprehensible might and power of the Creator of the universe.

Those who come to this quiet space are invited to such a greater awareness of God's presence in all of life.

Developing the Quiet Space

Please read "General Considerations," starting on page 92, before you begin.

ESSENTIALS

- Small space, private and quiet, indoors or out
- Bible
- Index cards with scriptures
- Writing table and chair
- Blank sheets of writing paper
- Pens or pencils
- Basket or container to hold writing paper, pens or pencils
- Five or so pictures (landscapes and people expressing emotions work particularly well) from magazines, such as *National Geographic* or *Newsweek*; or you may use personal photographs that have been enlarged.

- Small trash can
- Participant's Guide
- Sign to identify the quiet space: All of Life

OTHER POSSIBILITIES

- On a tabletop or flat surface, arrange items typically used in one's daily routine, such as a newspaper, a cookbook, cell phone, TV remote control, car keys, DVD, ball cap.

PROCEDURE

- Arrange an inviting space with selected furniture.
- Open the Bible to Psalm 139.
- Prepare selections from "Appropriate Readings" (page 13) to place in the space.

- Laminate the pictures or photographs, or glue them onto construction paper of various colors.

- Turn pictures facedown and fan them out on a flat surface.

- If using commonplace items, put them on focus area with Bible. Try using small boxes, such as tissue or cereal boxes, to elevate the Bible and one or two items. Drape the entire surface with a sheet or other fabric before arranging the collection of items.

- Place the Bible in the center of the display at the highest elevation.

- Copy the Participant's Guide or adapt it to fit your needs.

- Post sign(s).

- Pray a blessing on this space and on all who come to it.

APPROPRIATE READINGS

- This book open to pages 10–11

- Psalm 139:11-12

- Ecclesiastes 3:1

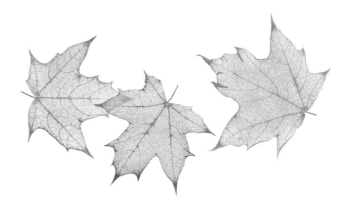

Participant's Guide: ALL OF LIFE

*O*ften we are awestruck at the evidence of God's handiwork. It is not difficult to recognize God when we witness the beauty of a sunset, hear the first cry of a newborn baby, or experience other joyous miracles of life. Still, at other times it seems nearly impossible for our untrained spirits to see past the pain, disappointment, loss, or uncertainty of life.

There is no place and no situation where God is not present. The psalmist perceived and expressed this reality in these familiar words addressed to God:

> Where could I go to escape your spirit?
> Where could I flee from your presence?
> If I climb the heavens, you are there,
> there too, if I lie in Sheol.
>
> If I flew to the point of sunrise,
> or westward across the sea,
> your hand would still be guiding me,
> your right hand holding me.
> —Psalm 139:7–10, JB

C. S. Lewis said, "The world is crowded with Him [God]. He walks everywhere *incognito*." [1] Learning to recognize God's presence in all of life—in pain as well as pleasure, in disappointment as well as fulfillment, in fear as well as peace—requires discipline, a discerning heart, and a keen sensitivity to the Holy Spirit.

You are invited to:

- Find the pictures lying facedown. Without looking at them, choose one picture. Keep it facedown on your lap or the table.

- Pray to be shown God's presence in the picture and for a willingness to be guided to anything God may want you to see.

- Now look at your picture. Take a few moments to contemplate what you see.

Now ask yourself the following questions:

- What story might this picture be telling?

- What do the eyes of my heart see in this picture?

- Where do I see Christ in this picture?

- What is Christ saying in general through this picture?

- What does Christ want to do about this circumstance?

- What is Christ saying to me, personally, through this picture?

- What scripture, if any, comes to mind?

On one of the blank pieces of paper provided, write a note to God about what is on your heart right now.

When you are ready to leave, feel free to take with you the page you have written on. Please leave the pictures facedown where you found them.

As you leave, ask that you may see God more clearly each day in all of life.

CHAPTER 2

Art

Let the beauty of the LORD our God be upon us,
And establish the work of our hands for us;
Yes, establish the work of our hands.
—Psalm 90:17, NKJV

———

Who dares to ponder a life bereft
of art that lends to soul the voice
of canvas, wheel, chisel, loom,
fiber, clay, palette, stone?

The hands that yield for hungry eyes
a form or color that reveals
some trace of Beauty's spirit wild
are surely Mystery's hands of grace.

Overview

*H*umankind has always used art as a language of the soul, a way of expressing that for which there are no words. Artifacts from primitive societies include drawings, sculpture, and pottery that reveal both an appreciation of beauty and a creative spirit. These relics also include images and symbols apparently used in places of worship, evidence of our ancestors' awareness of unseen realities. Today, we still use art to express our deepest longings, sensitivities, and experiences of the divine.

Though art is birthed with hands and tools, it springs from the spiritual life of the artist and speaks to the inner life of those who view it. Art conveys something of its creator's turbulence, centeredness, harmony, rhythm, or sensitivity to realms of the spirit. It also speaks of the artist's intent—whether the piece was intended to be useful, was produced as an exhibition of skills, was designed for appeal to a current market, or was created to express an experience of the Holy. As you select art for a quiet space, take time to sense the message of each piece. If an artist's statement about a work is available, read it carefully.

Options for artwork for this quiet space are extensive; but the most accessible, appropriate piece probably will be a painting, sculpture, mosaic, tapestry, carving, or piece of pottery. Ideally, the work will enable viewers to sense the creative force that brought it into being and continues to work through each of us. Hopefully, it will also convey a message or inspiration specific to its form and artistry.

Those who come to this quiet space are invited to:

- view art as an expression of the soul and an interaction with the divine Creator;

- relate to art as a symbol of our cocreation of life.

Developing the Quiet Space

Please read "General Considerations," starting on page 92, before you begin.

The following plan uses pottery in the quiet space, but you can adapt the plan's format for use with any kind of art. If using an art form other than pottery, see Appendix 2. If you prefer that participants create rather than, or in addition to, viewing art, see Appendix 1 for guidance.

ESSENTIALS

- Indoor space large enough to exhibit the art and allow participants to respond to it.

- Artwork: a tall pottery pitcher

- Stand or table for displaying the art

- Chair, bench, or pew

- Participant's Guide

- Supplies for response activity: an attractive container to hold clay, enough lumps of clay (1½"–2" in diameter) for each participant to have one

- Bible

- Readings

- Table or other surface on which to place readings and supplies

- Moist towelettes for cleaning hands and surfaces

- Sign to identify the quiet space: Art

OTHER POSSIBILITIES

- Lamp or spotlight to highlight the art

PROCEDURE

- Choose and reserve space.

- Obtain art: Use a piece you own; borrow one from someone you know; get one from a library, gallery, art guild, or other source that loans or rents art; or purchase one.

- Plan a guided response. Consider the following:

  a) View the pitcher meditatively. What is its

place—its function—in the world? What does it say about its relationship with its creator? How are you and this vessel alike?

b) Take a piece of clay and, with eyes closed, work it for several minutes. Feel its texture and malleability. Consider what a human life and clay have in common.

c) Contemplate the forces that shape a life: What are they? Which ones do you most want to shape you? What choices make that shaping possible?

- Prepare selections from "Appropriate Readings" to place in the space.

- Copy the Participant's Guide or adapt it to fit your needs.

- Gather all supplies and equipment: see "Essentials" and "Other Possibilities" above.

- Arrange the setting.

- Post sign(s).

- Pray a blessing on the space and on all who come to it.

APPROPRIATE READINGS

- This book open to pages 16–17

- Ecclesiastes 3:1-8

- Psalm 19:14

- Psalm 104:33-34

- "Art speaks to us at a subliminal level, beyond and before words. It is a direct communion with the divine creative force and does not require words, although they may come into play. A color, shape or feeling "speaks" its own message. . . . I believe that it is in creating that we most directly encounter the divine energy and become 'co-creators.'"—Sylvia Everett[1]

- "Creativity belongs to the artist in each of us. To create means to relate. The root meaning of the word *art* is to fit together and we all do this every day. Not all of us are painters but we are all artists.

Each time we fit things together we are creating—whether it is to make a loaf of bread, a child, a day. . . . This energy, which we call 'making,' is the relating of parts to make a new whole. The result might be a painting, a symphony, a building. If the job is done well, the work of art gives us an experience of wholeness called ecstasy—a moment of rising above our feelings of separateness, competition, divisiveness 'to a state of exalted delight in which normal understanding is felt to be surpassed' (Webster's)."—Corita Kent and Jan Steward, *Learning by Heart: Teachings to Free the Creative Spirit* [2]

- "When we undertake to polish our shoes with such consciousness that the experience hints at the transcendent, then we are creating a work of art. When Genesis says we are made in the image and likeness of God, I think that our very similarity to God lies in our ability to create. We are like God when we use the matter the Creator has already given us and further shape it to become the instrument through which he blows his song."—Gertrud Mueller Nelson, *To Dance with God* [3]

- "For the Greeks, beauty and harmony were sacred revelations; beauty was always present when the gods were honored. Similarly, beauty is the Navajo designation for an alliance with the spirits and nature. Beauty, or *Tepheret*, is the very heart of the kabbalistic Tree of Life, the place where spirit and form meet, the site of the connection between the divine and the earthly."—Deena Metzger, *Writing for Your Life* [4]

- "Creativity is a shapechanger. One moment it takes this form, the next that. It is like a dazzling spirit who appears to us all, yet is hard to describe for no one agrees on what they saw in that brilliant flash. Are the wielding of pigments and canvas, or paint chips and wallpaper, evidence of its existence? How about pen and paper, flower borders on the garden path, building a university? Yes, yes. Ironing a collar well, cooking up a revolution? Yes. Touching with love the leaves of a plant, pulling down 'the big deal,' tying off the loom, finding one's voice, loving someone well? Yes. Catching the hot body of the newborn, raising a child to adulthood, helping raise a nation from its knees? Yes. Tending to a marriage like the orchard it is, digging for psychic gold, finding the shapely word, sewing a blue curtain? All are of the creative life."—Clarissa Pinkola Estés, *Women Who Run with the Wolves*[5]

Participant's Guide: ART

*R*ead from the scriptures and other quotations placed within this space.

View the pitcher meditatively. Move around it; look at it from different perspectives.

What is its place, its function, in the world?

What does it say about the person who shaped it?

How are you and this vessel alike?

Take a piece of clay and work with it for several minutes.

Press, squeeze, pull, fold it.

Feel its texture and malleability. Don't consciously try to shape it; simply let your hands work with it.

Now close your eyes, work the clay, and think about what a human life and clay have in common.

Open your eyes and again look at the pitcher. (Continue to work the clay without focusing on it.) Contemplate the forces that shape a life.

Which influences do you most want to shape you?

What choices will make that possible?

What is your prayer for the you that you are co-creating?

Stay as long as you like. When ready to leave this space, look at your clay.

Does its shape bring anything to mind?

Feel free to take the clay with you, or shape it into a ball and return it to the container.

Please return this guide and the readings to their places and leave all in good order.

CHAPTER 3

Believing Power

Whoever believes in Him will not be disappointed.
—Romans 10:11, NASB

—⟋⟍—

The wounds that scar the mind and heart,
the pain that binds the soul,
the power of faith that transcends thought,
the Love that frees, makes whole,
all shape a life more certainly
than visible reality.

Overview

As the disciples were trained in faith building, Jesus explained that their faith would empower and equip them to be God's instruments of healing and other great works. When the disciples asked why they had been unable to heal a boy possessed by demons, Jesus responded with some impatience: "Because you have so little faith. I tell you the truth, if you have faith as small as a mustard seed, you can say to this mountain, 'Move from here to there' and it will move. Nothing will be impossible for you" (Matt. 17:20, NIV).

Jesus' promise was not limited to these twelve disciples. In Matthew 9:20-22 we see the fulfillment of the promise in the story about a determined woman, desperate from years of uncontrollable bleeding, whose faith in Jesus was strong. She believed that if she could simply touch the cloak Jesus wore, she would be healed. Acting on her faith, she reached out, daring to cross cultural boundaries, and instantly received healing.

Logic and modern science dominate the culture in the U.S. and other developed countries, leaving little, if any, room for the unexplained. In addition, a strong instinct for fair play can lead to an assumption about prayer: if one prayer is answered according to the desire of the one praying, then all prayers should be so answered. Because not all prayers are answered in the way we wish, we sometimes doubt that God has responded at all. We are skeptical of what we do not understand, and at best we seem to echo the words of the father of the demon-possessed boy who confessed, "I do believe; help me overcome my unbelief!" (Mark 9:24, NIV).

Those who come to this quiet space are invited to reach out to Christ our healer by imagining themselves in the story of the woman who believed Jesus could heal her great need.

Developing the Quiet Space

Please read "General Considerations," starting on page 92, before you begin.

ESSENTIALS

- A private, small space indoors or outdoors under a covered shelter
- Access to a working electrical outlet if possible
- Good lighting for reading
- Chair (or bench with a back)
- Table
- Bible
- Enough pieces of cloth for the number of people expected to visit this space
- Basket or container to hold cloth
- Participant's Guide
- Index cards

OTHER POSSIBILITIES

- Scriptures and other readings (see "Appropriate Readings")
- Picture of Jesus healing or talking to someone who is sick or in trouble. For possibilities, see http://clipart.christiansunite.com/Pictures_of_Jesus_Clipart/Healing_the_Sick_Clipart/
- Candle; tablecloth; items related to healing, such as prescription bottle, thermometer, ice pack
- CD player
- An audiotaped guided meditation for participants. See Appendix 3 for script and instructions.
- Sign to identify the quiet space: Believing Power

PROCEDURE

- Choose and reserve space.
- Prepare selections from "Appropriate Readings" to place in the space.
- Copy the Participant's Guide or adapt it to fit your needs.

- Obtain and prepare cloth: cut white, beige, or brown muslin into one-square-yard pieces. Roll up each piece and stand on end in a basket or other container. Provide enough pieces for each participant to keep one.

- Decorate the table with fabrics in hues of greens and blues, colors associated with healing.

- Place the Bible near the table or candle; open it to Matthew 9:20-22.

- If you have chosen additional scriptures or readings, print or type them on index cards.

- Post signs.

- Pray a blessing on this space and on all who come to it.

APPROPRIATE READINGS

- This book open to pages 24–25

- Luke 11:9-10

- 1 John 5:14-15

- Mark 11:24

- "Life has the power to make us stumble and, sometimes, to knock us off our feet. When life doesn't make sense, we have to decide what we will do about prayer."—Steve Harper, *Talking in the Dark: Praying When Life Doesn't Make Sense*[1]

- "You never know how much you really believe anything until its truth or falsehood becomes a matter of life and death to you."—C. S. Lewis, *A Grief Observed*[2]

Participant's Guide: BELIEVING POWER

The Gospels are filled with stories of how Jesus healed those who had faith in him. Sometimes Jesus sought out those he healed; at other times the sick, the lame, and those who desired healing for another went to great lengths to come into his healing presence.

Matthew 9:20-22 recounts the story of one woman whose faith was so remarkable that simply by reaching out through a great crowd to touch the Healer's garment, she instantly received healing from a blood disease that had plagued her for years. According to the account in Luke (8:46), Jesus felt the healing power leave him and acknowledged that the woman's faith had healed her.

Faith and prayer are as central to Christianity as heartbeat and breath are to life. However, the faith of the strongest Christian often will be challenged when struggling with unanswered prayer.

God's Word repeatedly instructs us to pray. But are the prayers of a righteous person still as powerful and effective today as they were during the centuries when the Bible was written? If God's Holy Word is relevant for today, how does the Christian explain unanswered prayers that have been offered faithfully in the belief that God will answer them?

In his book *Talking in the Dark*, author and prayer teacher Steve Harper speaks of his own struggle with unanswered prayer. He describes prayer as both mysterious and real; and he states, "You can have a prayer life and choose to avoid the mysteries. Or you can include the mysteries in your praying, knowing that even when you do, some will remain."[3]

Meanwhile, in the face of our own unanswered prayers, we continue to hear of people whose prayers have been answered miraculously. In such times, we may do well to remember the words of the father in Mark 9:24 (NASB) who confessed, "I do believe; help my unbelief." When this is the best we can truthfully say, we find it is all that's needed.

You are invited to:

Choose a piece of fabric from the basket.
Place it on your lap.

*Read the story found in Matthew 9:20–22 from the
Bible placed in this space for you.
Read the story again, this time more slowly.*

Try to imagine yourself as the one in the crowd
intent on reaching out to Jesus for healing.

As you hold the piece of cloth, name an area of
your life that needs the healing touch of Jesus.

While you consider this area of your life, place
the cloth on a part of your body that symbolizes the
location of your pain or brokenness.
*(For example, if you need healing from negative
thoughts, you might cover your head with the cloth. If you
need relational or emotional healing, hold the cloth close
to your heart or stomach.)*

In your mind, go back to the story of the woman
who reached out to touch Jesus' garment. Watch as
Jesus turns around and sees that you are the one who
has touched his cloak this time. Hear the kindness and
authority in Jesus' voice saying, *"Take heart, my child;
your faith has made you well."*

Let these words soak into your being. Enter into
conversation with Jesus if you wish. Stay in this
moment as long as you like.

Expect God to respond to your need as surely as
Jesus responded to the woman with the blood disease. Your prayers may be answered exactly as you
have asked, or the response may come about in an
entirely different way. Trust that God will respond
according to your need at this time and that God's
timing is perfect for you.

*Take a few moments to rest in the mystery of prayer
and of God's deep love for you.*

When you are ready to leave, you may take your
piece of cloth as a reminder that the Healer has heard
your cry, feels your pain, and knows your need.

As you leave, go in peace and in renewed faith.

CHAPTER 4

Bread and Juice

Are you able to drink the cup that I am about to drink?
—Matthew 20:22

Bread and juice,
born of grain and fruit,
essential elements
of life,
how fitting
that you represent
the essence of,
the life, the love,
of Christ.
Come now and feed
my body, soul;
come now, infuse
the hungry whole
of me.

Overview

When we think of everyday meals, we think of food from the earth and of the labor required to plant, harvest, and prepare it. When we consider time we share with others at table, our thoughts turn to the complexities of human relationships and to words, behaviors, and attitudes exchanged. All these shape who we are.

When we think of the Eucharistic meal, our focus moves from the visible to the invisible, and we realize that from this table we view life differently. We see earth's provisions as expressions of its Creator, and we see our lives as part of a much larger picture. We sense that this table symbolizes the communion of spirit with Spirit, the relationship in which we mortals draw closest to Truth. What happens here also profoundly shapes who we are.

In Jesus we recognize one who feasted in both the physical and the spiritual dimensions of reality. His perspective on the physical realm was enlightened by his time at table with the one he called Abba. Within that relationship he listened and learned, then he lived with such obedience and discernment that many say, "Just look at him! He's the spittin' image of his father."

Even as he died, Jesus' perspective remained constant. He had taught that it's right to love our enemies; in the agony of a torturous death, he prayed for God to forgive his tormentors. They did not, he said, know what they were doing (Matt. 5:44; Luke 23:34). That statement may have seemed foolish to his hearers, but future generations would learn that behaviors often derive from unconscious fears and desires and that love is the most effective agent of change.

Jesus chose elements of a meal to symbolize his life and death. The cup brings to mind the cup he drank and challenges us to drink—a life that blends agonies and ecstasies of relationship with the earth, with its inhabitants, and with the eternal Mystery. The bread reminds us of the essence of his life—his love, mercy, wisdom, and steadfast commitment—that we're invited to take within ourselves. Its breaking symbolizes the breaking of Jesus' body by the fear, lack of understanding, and thirst for power that blinded his killers.

Those who come to this quiet space are invited to:

- reflect on what writers have said about communion with the Holy;

- eat bread, drink juice, and invite a heightened sense of the sacred.

Developing the Quiet Space

Please read "General Considerations," starting on page 92, before you begin.

ESSENTIALS

- An indoor room or chapel large enough to accommodate a comfortable seat and a table for the juice and bread

- Table

- Chair or pew

- A place to kneel—altar rail, kneeling bench, cushion on the floor

- Breads of various kinds (for example, English muffins, Mexican tortillas, French baguettes, Danish sweet rolls)

- Two or three choices of 100-percent fruit juice

- Bible and list of scriptures

- Other readings (see "Appropriate Readings")

- Plates for bread and pitchers for juice

- Covers for bread and juice—clear domes or pieces cut from heavy, clear plastic

- Napkins and cups

- Participant's Guide

- Trash can

- Sign to identify the quiet space: Bread and Juice

- Antibacterial cleanser for hands, if no sink is easily accessible

PROCEDURE

- Choose and reserve space.

- Prepare selections from "Appropriate Readings" to place in the space.

- Plan for storage of bread and juice and for replenishment of supplies on the table.

- Arrange setting.

- Prepare and post sign(s).

- Set out breads and identify each with a small sign.

- Pray a blessing on this space and on all who come to it.

APPROPRIATE READINGS

- This book open to pages 30–31

- Luke 22:17-20

- Luke 22:42

- "When Jesus asks his friends James and John, the sons of Zebedee, 'Can you drink the cup that I am going to drink?' he poses the question that goes right to the heart of . . . life as a human being. . . .

   "'Can you drink the cup? Can you empty it to the dregs? Can you taste all the sorrows and joys? Can you live your life to the full whatever it will bring?' . . .

   "But why should we drink this cup? There is so much pain, so much anguish, so much violence. Why should we drink the cup? Wouldn't it be a lot easier to live normal lives with a minimum of pain and a maximum of pleasure? . . .

   "Drinking the cup of life involves *holding*, *lifting*, and *drinking*. It is the full celebration of being human. . . .

   "Can we hold our life, lift our life, and drink it, as Jesus did?"—Henri J. M. Nouwen, *Can You Drink the Cup?* [1]

Participant's Guide: BREAD AND JUICE

Read one or more of the available readings silently, slowly, expectantly. Be open to what the words may say to you.

Select a piece of bread and pour yourself some juice. Before you eat or drink:

Sit in a comfortable place. Hold your cup and focus on the juice. Does it pulse with your heartbeat? *What, if anything, does the pulsing suggest about the connection between the human heart and the heart of God?*

Look at the bread. *What, if anything, does bread have to do with flesh? How is bread connected with physical life? with spiritual life?*

Eat, drink, and reflect

- on the readings you have selected
- on the grain and fruit, the forces of nature that brought them from seed to maturity, their role in the daily lives of people throughout the world
- on the hands that sowed and harvested the grain and fruit, prepared and transported the bread and juice you now consume
- on your place in the worldwide family of God
- on the symbolism Jesus gave to bread, wine, the cup, drinking, and eating

If you wish, kneel and pray your gratitude, wonder, confession, longing—whatever you feel most deeply.

As you leave this space, ponder in your heart your experience here.

Before departing, please put your cup and napkin in the trash can and return this guide and other materials to their places.

CHAPTER 5

Breath, Wind, Spirit

The wind blows where it chooses, and you hear the sound of it,
but you do not know where it comes from or where it goes.
So it is with everyone who is born of the Spirit.
—John 3:8

—m—

A breeze caresses
mortal skin,
and Spirit gently
moves within—
breath of life,
ruach, wind.

Overview

*P*owerful. Invisible. Beyond the bounds of birth, death, time. Irrepressible. Of—but more than—the essence of our being. Pervasive. Omnipresent in human experience. All these descriptive words and phrases apply to breath, wind, and spirit, words that are interchangeable translations of the Hebrew term *ruach*.[1] All are well-suited for imaging the presence and movement of the sacred in our lives.

In picturesque language, Ezekiel depicts the revitalization of Israel as breath bringing life to dry bones (Ezek. 37:9-11). In Acts, we read that the Spirit's Pentecostal visitation incorporated a sound "like the rush of a violent wind" (Acts 2:2). The book of Proverbs captures an aspect of the nature of God in the question "Who has cupped the wind in the hollow of his hands?" (Prov. 30:4, NEB). The writer of Psalm 139 exclaims, "Where can I go from your spirit? Or where can I flee from your presence?" (v. 7). The Gospel of John uses wind as a synonym for spirit (3:8) in relating an encounter between Jesus and Nicodemus. Clearly, biblical writers recognized both the literal and the metaphorical significance of *ruach*.

We do not know where breath, wind, and spirit come from or where they go, but we do know that our lives depend on them.

Those who come to this quiet space are invited to:

- become aware of *ruach*'s continuing, pervasive presence and power;

- be grateful for all that breath, wind, and spirit represent.

Developing the Quiet Space

Please read "General Considerations," starting on page 92, before you begin.

ESSENTIALS

- Quiet, secluded outdoor location, preferably with an attractive view

- A comfortable seat: a bench or chair; a rock, stump, or grassy spot with a natural backrest (a rock face or tree, for example). Consider needs of persons with physical challenges.

- Participant's Guide

- This book with a note: "You may find pages 36–37 helpful reading as you begin your time in this quiet space."

- Waterproof container for this book

- Sign to identify the quiet space: Breath, Wind, Spirit

PROCEDURE

- Choose and reserve a space.

- Copy the Participant's Guide or adapt it to fit your needs. Because it will be used outdoors, be sure to cover it with adhesive plastic.

- Prepare the note to accompany this book, insert it between the appropriate pages, and place the book in a waterproof container.

- Place the guide where it will be readily visible. Hang it nearby; place it on or near the participant's seat and secure it with a rock or other heavy object; or place it in the waterproof container with the book.

- Post sign(s).

- Pray a blessing on this space and on all who come to it.

Participant's Guide: BREATH, WIND, SPIRIT

Read the pages marked in *Contemplative by Design*.

Pay attention to the air that surrounds your body. Can you feel it on your skin? Do you see evidence of its presence? If you come here tomorrow, will it exhibit the same characteristics?

How far does the air extend in each direction?

Can you gather air in your arms? If you were asked to "measure . . . a bushel of wind" (2 Esdras 4:5, NEB), what would you reply?

For several minutes, consider your breathing.
From where does your breath come?
Where does it go?
Is the breath yours, or is the universe in a sense breathing you as you breathe it?

Are you sharing breath with plants and trees? with other species of animals? with persons of differing gender, age, sexual orientation, race, political views, religious views, cultures?

Are you, in fact, sharing breath with peoples of other lands, other periods of history?

Now, inhale and hold your breath until it becomes uncomfortable to do so.
Exhale; then inhale the gift that awaits you.

Now return to regular breathing, aware that: *Breath is bearing oxygen to every cell of your body. The gift of life is given with every breath.*

If you feel inclined, pray as you breathe:

- *as you inhale,* "For breath, wind, spirit."
- *as you exhale,* "Thank you."

As you go from this place, continue to be mindful of the wonder of breath, wind, and spirit.

Please return this guide to its place and leave all in good order.

CHAPTER 6

Daily Offerings

For where your treasure is, there your heart will be also.
—Matthew 6:21

—w—

All gifts I place on altars
were made from what You gave,
so nothing that I offer
is any thing You crave;
but in my act of giving,
vain ownership disclaimed,
my ego, bowed, confesses
it also bears Your name.

Overview

Our days are gateways for an endless parade of products. Some bear food or shelter. Others offer adornment, comfort, education, or entertainment.

Goods can, however, become seductive. We may then come to believe that ownership will satisfy deep desires. Acquisition may become our passion. When material goods are granted such devotion, they affect our judgment and self-esteem. We begin to equate material wealth with success. Conversely, if we have little, we consider ourselves failures.

Hundreds of years before psychology identified these dynamics and industry reinforced them, Jesus clearly understood their reality and power. He understood that we may not see our allegiance to property, and that freedom from its control requires a painful passage to self-awareness.

Matthew, Mark, and Luke all recount a story that reveals this truth. A rich and powerful young man on a serious spiritual quest had followed the guidance given him, but he sensed a barrier between him and his goal. In a courageous act that broke with tradition, he went to Jesus and asked how to gain eternal life, the life of the spirit. The master teacher started with what the young man knew and could affirm about himself—the keeping of the commandments. The man proclaimed his obedience. Jesus, perceiving the real problem, then spoke a startling challenge. He told the rich young man to give all he had to the poor. Like a scalpel in the hands of a skilled surgeon, those words exposed the man's difficulty. They revealed a truth that lay buried far beneath awareness: his real treasure was not what he thought it was. In fact, he was more devoted to his wealth than to the life of his spirit.

Biblical teachings call us to honor the eternal and to see goods as temporary assets to be used responsibly.

Those who come to this quiet space are invited to:

- view everyday belongings with gratitude;

- place both goods and abilities in the service of a committed life;

- use their own words to complete a psalm of faith.

Developing the Quiet Space

Please read "General Considerations," starting on page 92, before you begin.

ESSENTIALS

- Small room or chapel, or an area within a larger space adequate to accommodate a display of items.

- Altar or table

- A collection of items that represent everyday activities and interests (examples: books, pencils, toys, hammer, trowel, vacuum brush, pots, pans, ballet shoes, musical instruments, DVDs, art supplies, music)

- Tabletop easels, boxes, or platforms to vary the levels of items in the arrangement

- Bible and list of scriptures

- Copies of "My Psalm" (page 44)

- Pencils or pens

- Clipboard or other writing surface

- Participant's Guide

- Table or other surface near entrance on which to place "My Psalm" sheets, pens or pencils, and Participant's Guide

- Containers for "My Psalm" and pencils (a box lid can work for the papers)

- Sign to identify the quiet space: Daily Offerings

PROCEDURE

- Choose and reserve space.

- Collect items that symbolize everyday activities. A variety of shapes, colors, and heights will enhance the arrangement.

- Prepare enough copies of "My Psalm" for expected number of participants.

- Prepare selections from "Appropriate Readings" to place in the space.

- Copy the Participant's Guide or adapt it to fit your needs.

- Gather remaining supplies and equipment (see Essentials above).

- Arrange the setting: items on table or altar, Bible, list of scriptures, clipboard, seating, table at entrance with Participant's Guide, copies of "My Psalm," pencils and pens.

- Prepare and post sign(s).

- Pray a blessing on this space and on all who come to it.

APPROPRIATE READINGS

- Mark 12:42-44

- Luke 18:18-27

- Mark 12:28-34

- This book open to pages 40–41

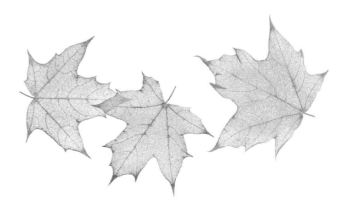

MY PSALM

O God, you are my refuge and my source. Who can compare with you?

You are _____,

you are _____, and I praise your holy name.

I have seen the beauty of your handiwork in _____

and _____, and I lift my thanks to you.

You have blessed me, in my making, with _____

and _____, and through your love

you help me to _____.

I bow before you in gratitude. I want to praise you with my life,

serve you with all I have, but I am weak and needy.

Forgive me when I _____,

and help me to _____.

Accept now, I pray, my _____ that I submit to your will.

You alone can _____.

You alone are my God. Amen.

When you have completed this page, read it aloud prayerfully. You may take your psalm with you when you leave.

Participant's Guide: DAILY OFFERINGS

In the Bible provided, look up Mark 12:42-44; Luke 18:18-27; and Mark 12:28-34. Read each passage slowly and thoughtfully.

Now focus on the items in the display. When one item draws your attention, ask what it represents for you:

Does it speak of a leisure activity? of responsibility at work or home? of something you enjoy or would like to do? something you do not enjoy?

Lift the item, hold it, turn it, feel it. Give free rein to your thoughts and emotions.

Do you feel troubled? resentful? pleased? sad? hopeful? inspired? Try to name your feelings.

Return the item to its place.

Offer all this item represents to you, consecrating that aspect of your life—positive or negative—to divine will.

Seek release of any need for control over what you have offered. Literally open your hands before God in a gesture of release.

Spend whatever time you need for reflection. When ready, read "My Psalm" completely before you fill the blanks. Thoughtfully complete the page; let the psalm serve as your closing prayer.

Before you leave this space, please return the Bible, readings, clipboard, guide, pen or pencil to their places.

CHAPTER 7

Deepening Silence

"Be still, and know that I am God!"
—Psalm 46:10

—ɯ—

The self in silence
yearns to know,
to dance, be free
of fetters round her feet;
but 'til she learns
to listen with her soul,
she never will
cast off her bonds,
she will not hear
the Great I Am,
she never will be whole.

Overview

Most of us are not aware of the controlling power of our habitual mannerisms, routines, and ways of processing information. If, however, we hope to become new creations, we probably will need to deal with habits that present barriers to change.

For example, an aversion to silence can keep us from spiritual encounters that are powerful agents of transformation. Lulled by days that hum with voices, traffic, and work, we grow accustomed to noise, and we automatically turn on radio, TV, or music in an attempt to avoid stillness. When we do, we eliminate periods of reflection that promote mental and emotional health. We also mute the still, small voice of God.

But silence alone does not assure awareness of the sacred. Meaningful silence is far more than absence of noise. It is a state of receptivity that invites spiritual manna. Silence itself does not create the feast, but the discipline of returning to silence again and again, letting it seep into bone and soul, opens the self to the Mystery at the core of the universe.

There are countless paths to awareness of the sacred. Other quiet spaces in this book offer guidance along paths of focused attention. The aim of this space is emptying ourselves of focus or goal, moving beyond thought to being, listening to the "sound of sheer silence" heard by Elijah (1 Kings 19:12). To experience this kind of silence, we must acquire the habit of availability. Even though we may feel nothing has changed in us, something undetectable will have happened within. This is the way of deepening silence.

Those who come to this space are invited to:

- empty themselves of thought and seeking;

- release themselves to the One in whom they live and move and have their being (Acts 17:28).

Developing the Quiet Space

Please read "General Considerations," starting on page 92, before you begin.

ESSENTIALS

- A small, quiet, sparsely furnished room (If you must use a portion of a larger area, use room dividers to define the space.)

- Small table with lamp for soft lighting

- Seating options: a chair and a floor cushion

- Participant's Guide and a timer that can be set for minutes

- Slips of paper, pencils, a small covered box with slot in its lid (for the offering of concerns)

- Sign for entrance; printed on one side: "Please wait. Space in use." On the flip side: "Space available. Come in."

- Sign to identify the quiet space: Deepening Silence

OTHER POSSIBILITIES

- Sheer fabric (fabric remnants or sheer curtain panels from an outlet store) to drape a doorway, window, or portion of wall

- Small icon or other piece of art for the table

- A small fountain to cover background sounds

PROCEDURE

- Choose and reserve space and obtain permission, if needed, to make changes, such as hanging fabric and removing furniture or pictures.

- Copy the Participant's Guide or adapt it to fit your needs.

- Cover a small box (checkbook box, for instance) with adhesive paper and cut a slit in its top.

- Post sign(s). Place occupancy sign on doorknob or nearby.

- Arrange the space:
  > Remove clutter or extraneous furniture.
  > If using fabric, hang it over an open doorway, over a window, or on a wall.
  > Position table, lamp, chair, cushion, and perhaps art. If including a fountain, place it where splatters will do no damage.

  > Place the box, papers, and pencils for the "offering of concerns" on or near the table.
  > Place guide and timer on the chair.

- Pray a blessing on this space and on all who come to it.

Participant's Guide: DEEPENING SILENCE

*T*urn the sign at the entrance to indicate this space is in use.

If you are burdened with a problem or question likely to distract you, write it on a slip of paper, offer it into God's care, and place the paper in the box provided. (Papers will later be burned, unread.)

Seat yourself either in the chair or on the floor cushion. Set the timer for fifteen or twenty minutes. Assume a comfortable position with back straight and hands open, resting in your lap.

Do not seek a specific solution or answer to problems or questions.

Seek only to open completely to the One in whom you live and move and have your being.

Breathe regularly. Quiet your inner clamor.

Do not fight thoughts that arise, but don't hold onto them either. Release them with no appraisal, and return to openness.

You may find it helpful to:

- Consider inner turbulence as the sea to which Jesus said, "Peace, be still."

- When thoughts bubble up, think, "Peace," and let go of them.

- Close your eyes and continue this exercise until the timer sounds.

As you leave, take with you a deepened sense of serenity.

Please return the guide and timer to their places and turn the sign outside the door to read: "Space available. Come in."

CHAPTER 8

Flame and Dance

For everything there is a season,
and a time for every matter under heaven:
. . . .
a time to weep, and a time to laugh;
a time to mourn, and a time to dance.
—Ecclesiastes 3:1, 4

Dance
opens doors
to mystic realms
in which we're free
to soar . . .
and celebrates
the mysteries,
the energies,
the miracles of life.

Overview

Fire is in constant motion—swaying, bending, reaching, changing in response to an unseen breath or current of wind. Life too is a dance. In our relationship with God, we move forward, backward, left, and right, sometimes with rhythmic grace, sometimes resisting the One who would lead us. In relationships with family and friends, our choices, thoughts, and actions complement others or inflict pain; we move in harmony, or we step on toes.

Both flame and mortal depend on breath, wind, and spirit for life and direction; and both affect their environment in surprisingly similar ways. A flame can warm, transform, consume, or destroy. Humans dispense warmth, contribute to transformation, or wreak havoc, depending on which spirit most moves us. *Spirit* can be defined as "the activating . . . principle influencing a person."[1] In this sense, the spirits that influence us will include—among many—rage, grief, compassion, fear, and love. As we dance our days, it is important to recognize our partners.

Moving the physical body to express inner experience provides a way to offer the experience into God's light and love. In so doing, we may see it more clearly. We can dance our joy, anger, frustration, pleasure, hope, despair, gratitude, sense of abandonment—any feeling whatsoever. We can also dance our praise, supplication, intercession, confession, and commitment.

Biblical writings encourage us to bare our inner selves to God, and they validate dance as a means of doing so. Scripture records every possible emotion, and beginning in Exodus (15:20-21) with Miriam and her tambourine, we see that men and women have danced their feelings and their worship through the centuries.

Those who come to this quiet space are invited to:

- meditate on the movement of a flame;

- ponder scripture and other writings;

- move in ways that express emotion and prayer.

Developing the Quiet Space

Please read "General Considerations," starting on page 92, before you begin.

ESSENTIALS

- A space large enough for movement—indoors or outside in an open shelter with covering
- Oil lamp or sturdy candleholder with candles and protective globe[2]
- Candlelighter
- Candlesnuffer
- Readings
- CDs and player
- Participant's Guide
- Table or other surface on which to place the items listed (allow generous space around the candle or lamp)
- Basket of scarves and small percussion instruments, such as shakers
- Chair, bench, or floor cushions
- Sign to identify the quiet space: Flame and Dance
- Bag of sand or bucket of water for extinguishing fire if necessary

PROCEDURE

- Choose and reserve space.
- Check policies and get permission, if needed, to have a lighted lamp or candle in the chosen area.
- Plan for adequate supervision of the space. Have someone posted close by to add oil to the lamp regularly or replace candles and be sure all is safe.
- Prepare selections from "Appropriate Readings" to place in the space.
- Copy or adapt the Participant's Guide. Definitely laminate if the space will be outdoors.
- Post sign(s).
- Place a bag of sand and/or bucket of water where it is clearly visible.

- Pray a blessing on this space and on all who come to it.

Offer a variety of musical styles in this space, including different moods, rhythms, and instrumentation. Before including a CD, listen to it and move to it. If you don't have what you need, visit a good music store or ask a dancer or dance instructor for recorded music suggestions.

APPROPRIATE READINGS

- 2 Samuel 6:14

- Psalm 150:4-6

- Luke 15:25

- This book open to pages 52–53

- "When they ask what happened here,
  We'll simply say
  Christ came by and we learned his dance.
  . . . .
  The Lord does his dance with all the wrong people:

With slaves and lepers and tax collectors,
With cursing fishermen and adulterers and thieves,
With outcasts and castoffs.
He dances with the unclean, with the orphan, with the displaced,
    with the unwhole.
And he won't dance with us,
No matter how plaintively we call
Lord, Lord . . .
He won't dance with us
Until we become
(Of all things)
As little children;
Until we admit we are the needy,
    we are the outcasts,
    we are the orphans.
Then he says to us:
    Come unto me!
    And we become the accepted unacceptables,
    Our brokenness is bound,
    And we are able to follow the dance."
—Ann Weems, *Reaching for Rainbows*[3]

- "Why dance the praise? So the words can be formed in the motion of the body. So the spirit emerges from the very cauldron, the heat and fire of the self."—Deena Metzger, *Writing for Your Life*[4]

- "If we left it to the Spirit, there would be only the Way and the celebrating. The Love and the alleluias. The Living and the joy. The Gift and the thank you. The Song and the singing. The Good News and the shouting. But do we believe it? We're given abundance and we complain. Every day is a birthday and we walk around lifeless. God gives us Light and we close our eyes. God hands us Christmas and we yawn. The miracle is that God is always there, not dwelling in our chaos and our deadness, but offering us change:

  Life—Joy—Song—Dance.

  What would it take to snap you awake?

  What would it take to make you alive and free to react, to respond, to live to God's music?

  Once there was a time when you danced. Remember? You weren't afraid to dance then.

  Once you could cry and laugh and dance and sing.

  Once you could be angry and direct your anger appropriately. Once you could love fiercely.

  'Unless you turn and become like children . . .'"
  —Ann Weems, *Reaching for Rainbows*[5]

Participant's Guide: FLAME AND DANCE

*L*ight the oil lamp. Sit quietly and focus on its dancing flame.

What does its movement bring to mind?

Why does the flame dance?

Do you feel any kinship with the flame?

If so, in what way?

Read the scripture and readings provided. After a period of silence, if you feel so inclined, let your body move—

with the flame or to some inner impulse, and, if you'd like, to a CD you select and play.

Don't worry about feeling inhibited. Ann Weems writes:

Are you a dancer who's never danced?

Are you a singer who's never sung?

Are you a laugher who holds it in?

Are you a weeper who's afraid to cry?

Are you someone who cares, but is afraid to risk love?

Do you have an alleluia deep inside you growing rusty?[*]

Let your feelings or prayer rise from within you and move your body to express praise, supplication, penitence, joy, anger, longing, sorrow, or alleluias—whatever you feel.

If you'd like, use one or more items from the basket as you dance.

As you move through days to come, be aware of your dance and of your partners.

Extinguish the flame before you leave.

Please return this guide to its place and leave all in good order.

[*] Ann Weems, *Reaching for Rainbows* (Louisville, KY: Westminster John Knox Press, 1980), 91.

CHAPTER 9

God's Rest

Come away by yourselves,
and we will go to a lonely place to get some rest.
—Mark 6:31, NCV

—⚬—

To rhythm's grand significance, its many roles attest:
the heart and lung, the body, mind and seasons of the earth,
constrict, release, expand, relax—or sleep, produce/give birth,
and each decisive, healthy beat depends, for life, on rest.
So honor well a plan devised by One more wise than we.

Overview

Just as the body needs regular rest in order to function properly, the spirit also requires and yearns for regular times of restful retreat in God's presence. We were created with a need to break from the activities of the day to spend time in quiet communion with God. Our overly packed agendas often push aside a desperate need for spiritual refueling and refreshing.

We suspect we are lazy if each minute is not filled with work-related or socially engaging activities. Even at church, with the best of intentions, we can fall into the trap of taking on too many tasks. Before long we may feel controlled or overwhelmed by the busyness of life.

Stress takes its toll. To keep up with the demands of life, some either start or end the day with a drink or an antianxiety drug. In *Through the Looking-glass*, Lewis Carroll states, "It takes all the running *you* can do, to keep in the same place."[1] This is all too true in today's world. We find wisdom in these words from an anonymous writer: "In bustle so little is accomplished. You must learn to take the calm with you in the most hurried days."[2]

One helpful thing we can do for ourselves or for someone else is to shine a light on some of the best gifts ever given to us: rest, renewal, and communion with God. Our spiritual health and inner joy pivot around these gracious gifts.

Those who enter this quiet space are invited to slow down and enter into God's rest for a few brief moments.

Developing the Quiet Space

Please read "General Considerations," starting on page 92, before you begin.

ESSENTIALS

- Small outside area
- Portable hammock or comfortable chair
- Participant's Guide
- Portable (battery-operated) CD player and headphones
- One or two CDs of soft music, free of familiar words, to help relax the body and mind. Two possibilities: *Agnus Dei: Music of Inner Harmony* by the Choir of New College Oxford and *Feather Light* by Hilary Stagg. Both these CDs are available at www.amazon.com.
- Sign to identify the quiet space: God's Rest

PROCEDURE

- Locate a space outside with peaceful and pleasant surroundings.
- Set up a hammock or comfortable chair.
- Copy Participant's Guide or adapt it to fit your needs.
- Post sign(s).
- Pray a blessing on this space and on all who come to it.

Participant's Guide: GOD'S REST

*B*reaking from the busyness of life to enter into rest is an important part of God's plan for us. This practice has been modeled for us in God's Word, the Bible. God rested from the work of creating the world. Adam and Eve ended the activities of each day to meet with God "in the cool of the day" (Gen. 3:8, NIV). God commanded that one day out of seven be given to holy sabbath rest. Jesus took time away from his work, the disciples, and the crowds to spend time alone with God.

God's Spirit continues calling us to lay aside work, step away from the noise of the world, and spend time in God's presence. Entering God's rest is a gift and privilege, and when we do so, our drained spirits are refueled.

You are invited to:
Accept the invitation simply to rest by lying in the hammock or relaxing in the chair provided for you.

To help you relax as you enter into God's rest, you may select and play a CD.

Take in the warmth of the sun or the shade of the day with your senses. If you feel a breeze, allow it to caress your body and soothe your soul.

If sounds have distracted you, let them gently fade into the background.

Give yourself permission to put aside concerns or recurring thoughts, knowing you can come back to them later if you like.

Know that God has called you here.

Silently offer praises to Christ, giving thanks for the gift of rest and renewal.

Be still now and allow God to minister to you in whatever way God chooses.

When you are ready, leave with the assurance that God's rest is available to nourish and renew you each day.

Please put this guide, the CD player, headphones, and CDs back where you found them.

CHAPTER 10

Life's Knots and Tangles

Do not be anxious about anything, but in everything,
by prayer and petition, with thanksgiving,
present your requests to God.
—Philippians 4:6, NIV

—⚒—

In a moment of time we came to be;
and in moments of time we're called to see
our trials more clearly, their web of turns,
the path we're on, its lessons learned.

Overview

Sometimes life seems to bring one difficulty or disappointment after another. It has been said that each person has either just come out of a crisis, is getting ready to go into a crisis, or is in the middle of a crisis. While this may be an exaggeration, certainly all of us have experienced something beyond our realm of understanding and control. Going through a crisis can make us stronger, but there are also times when we seem to crumble under the weight.

We can encounter what at first appears to be a fairly small problem. Then somehow it becomes overwhelming as we attempt to fix it on our own. Such a circumstance is like tangles or knots that become tighter and more complicated as we struggle to sort them out.

This quiet space offers time for introspection, for prayers of intercession or petition, and perhaps for relinquishing control of a problem. The setting provides an opportunity for participants to hold on to something tangible that has been knotted or tangled and to name whatever is troublesome or confusing, while slowly unraveling the first knot in a series of tangles. More knots may be untangled while presenting each additional concern to God in prayer.

Developing the Quiet Space

Please read "General Considerations," starting on page 92, before you begin.

Please read "General Considerations," starting on page 92, before you begin.

ESSENTIALS

- Small and secluded space, either outdoors or indoors
- A bench, chair, swing, or glider
- A basket or other attractive container with pieces of tangled or purposely knotted yarn
- Participant's Guide
- Sign indicating quiet space: Life's Knots and Tangles

OTHER POSSIBILITIES

- A covered plastic container if materials will be left outdoors

PROCEDURE

- Choose yarn in a variety of soft colors.
- Tie knots in the yarn or tangle the yarn.
- Wind the knotted yarn back into a ball or skein.
- Copy the Participant's Guide or adapt it to fit your needs.
- Post sign(s).
- Pray a blessing on this space and on all who come to it.

Participant's Guide: LIFE'S KNOTS AND TANGLES

I watched as my niece casually picked up the two necklaces tangled together in a series of impossible knots. I had long given up on separating them and was ready to send the mess to the trash bin.

Katie worked expertly as she unraveled tangle after tangle. Triumphantly, she soon handed over the two separate necklaces that I had been unable to wear for months. In a matter of a few minutes, my young niece taught me an important lesson about patience, determination, and asking for help.

A major problem or even a small hiccup in life can turn into what feels and looks like a tightly pulled knot or a series of difficult tangles. Most of us have experienced a time when we have had to sit back and allow someone with a fresh approach or expert hands to help us in our struggles.

Are you or someone you know facing a difficult situation to which there appears no solution or way out? Silently name that person or situation.

You are invited to:

- Take a piece of yarn from the basket.

- Find the first knot, and, as you think about the person or situation you named, slowly and patiently begin the process of unraveling the tangle.

- As you untangle the yarn, pray for God's hope-filled peace to come to the individual you have named and for God's clear guidance and healing power in this situation.

Visualize yourself placing this person or circumstance into God's strong and capable hands. Feel the heaviness being lifted off you as you leave this situation with the One whose loving hands can unravel all the knots and tangles in our lives.

Take a deep breath and hold it a few seconds. As you exhale, allow your body and your mind to relax as you offer thanks to God.

Repeat this process as often as you wish.

CHAPTER 11

Life's Mysterious Center

Stand at the crossroads and look;
ask for the ancient paths,
ask where the good way is, and walk in it,
and you will find rest for your souls.
—Jeremiah 6:16, NIV

Round and round and round we turn—
earth spins us toward, then from, the sun,
we dance for joy, but then we mourn,
we live, we die, we are reborn—
and through it all, within our core,
there is a lodestar, centered, sure,
that draws us to its heart and then
commends us to our path again.

Overview

During the Middle Ages, walking a labyrinth could substitute for a long, often dangerous pilgrimage to a place of religious significance. Pilgrimages were deemed important because the church taught that prayers made in the Holy Land or at the burial site of a saint were sure to be heard and looked upon with favor. Though seldom used today in place of a long spiritual journey, the labyrinth still draws spiritual seekers to walk its metaphoric path to the mysterious center of God's heart and then retrace their steps to return to everyday life.

The labyrinth, a main feature of many cathedrals since the twelfth century, holds a fascination for us in the twenty-first century. Most labyrinths used by Christians today are patterned after the labyrinth at Chartres Cathedral in northern France, one of the few surviving labyrinths from the medieval period. Other variations include classical, Santa Rosa, and neo-medieval labyrinths.

Whatever the style, labyrinths offer spiritual benefits for Christians now as in earlier times. Since time began, men and women searching for answers to life's questions have been drawn into contemplative reflection. In the noise and rush of life today, the labyrinth appeals to many as a respite from daily cares and schedule overload, affording a window for contemplation. But even stronger than the human yearning to get away from it all is the inner beckoning of the Holy Spirit to "come with me by yourselves to a quiet place" (Mark 6:31, NIV). For those who are willing to slow down and to commune with God, walking a labyrinth can be like a drink of cool water on a hot day.

The purpose of this quiet space is to remind us that:

- God walks the path of life with us.

- God also waits to greet us when we arrive at life's mysterious center.

Developing the Quiet Space

Please read "General Considerations," starting on page 92, before you begin.

ESSENTIALS

- A level indoor or outdoor space large enough for the labyrinth you will be using

- A labyrinth

- Participant's Guide

- Sign to identify the quiet space: Life's Mysterious Center

OTHER POSSIBILITIES

- CD of soft, meditative music (The music of Taizé is widely used for walking the labyrinth. One example is *Alleluia* by Jacques Berthier, GIA Publications.)

- Portable (battery-operated) CD player with headphones

- Live music (consider a guitarist, harpist, or string quartet for a special event)

- Candles if evening walks are an option

- A sign indicating when the labyrinth is open for general use and another to post when hosting specific groups. ("Welcome to all who desire to enter the threshold of the labyrinth's path." Or, "This labyrinth is temporarily reserved for [name of group] on [date and time]. It will be open again for public use on [day, date, and time]. We apologize for any inconvenience.")

PROCEDURE

- Determine the location for the labyrinth.

- If using an indoor labyrinth, purchase, rent, borrow, or design and make your own portable labyrinth. Some companies will sell their older-style or well-worn rentals at a discount. (To purchase or rent, see www.labyrinthcompany.com.)

- If hiring someone to build an outdoor labyrinth, determine the style you want and begin looking for a reputable company with good prices.

- If you plan to create your own outdoor labyrinth, find detailed plans that suit your needs. Ask for suggestions from others who have built their own labyrinths. Find volunteers to help. (For instructions on building your own labyrinth, see www.ehow.com/how_2074956_ create-labyrinth. html.)

- For those who cannot walk a labyrinth, finger labyrinths small enough to be placed on a desk, table, or bedside are available (see www.labyrinthcompany.com).

- If using live music, decide what kind of music would be best and research local musicians (such as, harpists, guitarists, woodwind players). Select music conducive to the peacefulness of the labyrinth.

- Consider having a dedication ceremony once the labyrinth is completed or when the portable labyrinth arrives. Plan for a time of general instructions and history of the labyrinth as part of the ceremony.

- Copy Participant's Guide or adapt it to fit your needs. You may choose to give each participant an individual guide with suggested prayers or scriptures (Ps. 23:4; Isa. 2:3; John 8:12). Or you may simply post a permanent or semipermanent guide near the labyrinth's entrance with instructions and a bit of history for all to read before beginning their journey.

- Post sign(s).

- Pray a blessing on this space and on all who come to it.

Participant's Guide: LIFE'S MYSTERIOUS CENTER

The labyrinth is steeped in the ancient Christian practice of seeking God to find meaning to life and answers to problems. Christians find strong spiritual symbolism in the labyrinth. Following the labyrinth's paths, the traveler makes several 180-degree turns before reaching the center. This metaphor for our life journey prepares the heart and opens the mind to the presence of Christ, who is not only taking each step with the pilgrim but waiting at the center for the pilgrim's arrival.

In preparation for walking the labyrinth, take a few moments to reflect on your life. Consider your relationships, difficulties, questions, new directions, or whatever else you may bring here. Pray for help in setting aside any cares or concerns, so that you can experience God in this moment.

Keep in mind that each labyrinth journey—walking along the path and reaching the center—will bring a new experience. Perhaps you unexpectedly will be filled with joy, kick off your shoes, and skip along the path with the freedom of a child. You may be moved to tears by your love for God, for others, and for the world. Your experience may be somber, characterized by deep thoughts or intimate conversations with God.

As you begin, please be mindful that the labyrinth walk is a shared activity. Others may be in the labyrinth at the same time you are. Each person will travel at his or her own pace, so please be considerate and share the path.

When you reach the center, which represents the heart of God, you may spend as much time as you like there. Take in the moment, the feelings, thoughts, words; take in all that God offers you.

As you leave the center, retrace your steps to the starting point. When you complete your labyrinth journey, you may discover a newfound energy and be filled with insights and discoveries about yourself, God, or the world.

If you do not experience any of these things, do not be discouraged or feel you have somehow failed. We all come with our individual personalities and unique ways of communing with God. For some, walking the gentle labyrinth path may simply be a way to escape the noise and rush of everyday life by spending time in peaceful silence. This in itself is a welcome experience.

As you reflect on this practice that has been shared by Christians for hundreds of years, give thanks for whatever gift you, and others throughout the ages, have received by walking the labyrinth.

CHAPTER 12

Love's Sacrifice

For God so loved the world
that he gave his one and only Son.
—John 3:16, NIV

—⁊⁊⁊—

Through you I glimpse the scope of Love:
present from the beginning of time,
manifest in humankind
constant, sure, when cursed, reviled,
forgiving, still, when crucified,
and leaving me with no excuse
to say I'm only human,
no reason to refuse the cup
or bread of life I'm given.

Overview

Surely nothing has been more thought of, sought after, argued about, or cherished than love. The foundation of Christian belief is love. But though the truth of love appears throughout the Bible, the concept is frequently elusive and misunderstood.

Too often what we call love is actually self-centeredness played out in ways that harm the so-called beloved. Both individuals and groups can use this false love for personal gain. Sadly, even the church sometimes acts out of such misunderstanding of love.

Jesus, our perfect example of love and God's perfect gift of love, was given to a selfish and imperfect people. We have been told and shown in many ways that God loves us. The most vivid enactment of that love is Jesus' sacrifice on the cross.

Just as the cross of Christ brings a paradox of bitter and sweet, love brings its own paradox in that we long to receive the very thing we must give. We have been created to both give and receive love. While doing either may appear to be natural and easy, the deeper dimension to real love always requires a sacrifice of either action or inaction. To mirror the love Jesus modeled for us is the most difficult yet important challenge a Christian will ever face.

Reflecting on the life and death of Christ stirs within us a deep need to look at ourselves. John Mogabgab, editor of *Weavings: A Journal of the Christian Spiritual Life*, says we are called to ask ourselves a question that is the true measure of success in life: *Have I loved well?*[1]

The purpose of this quiet space is to:

- look more deeply at God's sacrificial love;

- consider honestly the question *Have I loved well?*

Developing the Quiet Space

Please read "General Considerations," starting on page 92, before you begin.

ESSENTIALS

- Indoor or outdoor space that is private and quiet
- A cross—any size or material
- Box with letter-sized opening (Find a box with a hinged lid, or cover a cardboard tissue box.)
- Participant's Guide
- A comfortable place to sit
- Flat writing surface
- Strips of paper
- Pencils or pens
- Basket for paper and pencils
- Sign to identify the quiet space: Love's Sacrifice

OTHER POSSIBILITIES

- Bible
- Small, inexpensive crosses for each participant to take as a reminder of God's love (may be found at your local Christian supply store)
- Container for the crosses

PROCEDURE

- Place the sealed letter box near the cross.
- Cut paper or index cards into strips small enough to fit through the box opening. To ensure participants' privacy, empty the box periodically and burn notes without reading them.
- Copy the Participant's Guide or adapt it to fit your needs.
- Post sign(s).
- Pray a blessing on this space and on all who come to it.

Participant's Guide: LOVE'S SACRIFICE

The Bible tells us our two main responsibilities are to love God and to love others. Yet nothing is more difficult to do. It is easy to say we love God, and almost as easy to say we love others! But such words become meaningless when we realize that the love God requires, the same love Jesus modeled for us, calls for sacrifice. We often consider this too costly.

John Mogabgab, a Christian writer, has come to see that success in this world will boil down to a single, simple, and disturbingly profound question: *Have I loved well?* Truly loving well means different things to different people, but it always involves an element of sacrifice. The Cross reminds us of the sacrifice Jesus made by giving his life for those whom God loved so much.

Take a few moments to ask yourself the following questions. Answer each one as if you see Jesus sitting beside you. Next, ask Jesus to speak to you about your responses.

- *How has God's sacrificial love affected my life?*

- *Does God see me as one who loves well?*

- *How may I have failed to love God or others sacrificially?*

- *How is God calling me to a sacrificial love right now?*

Perhaps you feel the Holy Spirit prompting you to take some specific action. Using the paper and pencil provided, draw a symbol of what you need to do, or write a significant word or two or even a sentence about it.

When you have finished, place your response in the box provided near the cross. The responses will not be read by anyone but will be prayerfully burned at the end of the day.

CHAPTER 13

Nature

Before you mountains and hills shall break into cries of joy,
and all the trees of the wild shall clap their hands.
—Isaiah 55:12, NEB

—⁓—

Listen to the voice of the rainbow,
bend to morning sounds of the dew,
hear the gentle tones of the flowers,
their songs they will sing to you.

For you were created for hearing
their lyrics more lucent than speech
that come to you through the silence
to comfort, inspire, teach.

Overview

From Genesis on, the Bible invites us to see that the world around us reveals the sacred. One of the best known of such passages is:

> The heavens are telling the glory of God;
> and the firmament proclaims his handiwork.
> Day to day pours forth speech,
> and night to night declares knowledge.
> There is no speech, nor are there words;
> their voice is not heard;
> yet their voice goes out through all the earth,
> and their words to the end of the world.
> —Psalm 19:1-4

The Old Testament also contains stories in which animals convey messages to humans (see Gen. 3:1-5; Num. 22:28-30) and many verses that use nature vocabulary to poignantly reveal the complexity of human experience. Psalm 23's green pastures, still waters, and valley of the shadow of death beautifully capture the breadth and depth of life.

In the New Testament as well, nature speaks of both God and humankind. Jesus, clearly an avid student of the natural world, incorporated trees, fruits, branches, vines, logs, splinters, seeds, goats, sheep, and rocks into his stories and parables. Through him, these creations help us understand ourselves and our relationship to the Creator of all.

Consequently, contemporary seekers often use flowers, stones, leaves, or other gifts of nature to provide a focus during meditation. A single leaf can prompt consideration of life and death, our connection to our Source, the beauty and complexity of our days, and the significance of our place in the whole.

Precisely because nature is as common and essential to us as our own bone and flesh, we easily become blind to its revelations of the sacred.

Those who come to this quiet space are invited to:

- read what others have learned from nature;

- allow a gift from nature to speak to them;

- record their experience.

Developing the Quiet Space

Please read "General Considerations," starting on page 92, before you begin.

ESSENTIALS

- Space adequate to hold a display of gifts from nature (may be indoors or outdoors if display can be protected from the weather)

- Collection of nature's gifts, such as flowers, shells, polished stones, rocks, cones, seedpods, sticks, bark, fossils, gourds, leaves, moss

- Table or other surface on which to display the collection

- Comfortable place to sit

- Participant's Guide

- Newsprint pad (or newsprint mounted on a wall) and markers for recording responses

- Readings

- Sign to identify the quiet space: Nature

OTHER POSSIBILITIES

- Background music that includes nature sounds[1]

PROCEDURE

- Choose and reserve space.

- Prepare selections from "Appropriate Readings" to place in the space.

- Copy the Participant's Guide or adapt it to fit your needs.

- Collect items from nature.

- Arrange the setting. Enhance the display of nature's gifts by grouping them attractively. Leave empty space between groupings; place objects on napkins or mats; or position them at different levels on pedestals fashioned with variously sized boxes covered with fabric. For a large display, cover a collection of boxes with a tablecloth or sheet. Display the readings between groupings or on surfaces nearby.

- Post sign(s).

- Pray a blessing on this space and on all who come to it.

APPROPRIATE READINGS

- This book open to pages 76–77

- Psalm 148:9-10, 13

- "There is [a] . . . teacher, and she is the most profound teacher of them all. This teacher belongs to all of us and gives to us all equally, though we may not equally recognize her or accept her teachings. This teacher is, of course, nature. Nothing, no one, in the human realm compares to her. When we recognize nature as the ultimate teacher, we set aside the antics and aggrandizements of human ego that plague us increasingly.

  "Nature is what we come out of and descend into. The middle passage is what we call our lives, and in this realm between the source and the aftermath, between the roots and the highest branches of the World Tree, we often try to forget our origins and destiny as if we sprang out of air and could become air again through effort and deserving.

  "Nature teaches us otherwise, says we must get our hands dirty, says we are also fire, water, and earth. Says we have a body. Says that bodies matter. Says that the tree is equal to us, also the wolf and the stone. These teachings break us down; afterward, they allow us to see."
  —Deena Metzger, *Writing for Your Life*[2]

- "Love all God's creation, the whole and every grain of sand in it. Love every leaf, every ray of God's light. Love the animals, love the plants, love everything. If you love everything, you will perceive the divine mystery in things. Once you perceive it, you will begin to comprehend it better every day. And you will come at last to love the whole world with an all-embracing love . . . . Man, do not pride yourself on superiority to the animals; they are without sin, and you, with your greatness, defile the earth by your appearance on it, and leave the traces of your foulness after you—alas, it is true of almost every one of us!"
  —Fyodor Dostoyevsky, *The Brothers Karamazov*[3]

Participant's Guide: NATURE

*R*ead some or all the quotations displayed. Look at the collection of nature's gifts until you are drawn to a particular one.

Lift that item from the display.

Turn it. Feel it.

Let your thoughts about it roam freely.

After several minutes, ask yourself

the following questions:

- *How am I like this gift of nature? How am I different?*

- *What does the gift reveal about God? What does it say about life and death?*

- *Is the Creator speaking to me in some way through this creation?*

When you are ready, return the item to its place in the display. If you feel drawn to do so, repeat the steps above with another item.

When so inclined, go to the newsprint and use markers to express your feelings, thoughts, or a prayer. Draw an image or symbol, write words or sentences, or simply use splashes of color.

As you leave this space, go with senses more finely tuned to the beauty and wonder of the world that sustains you. You may leave the newsprint page or take it with you.

Please return this guide to its place and leave everything in order.

CHAPTER 14

Spiritual Family Tree

The LORD God said, "It is not good for the man to be alone."
—Genesis 2:18, NIV

—⟋⟍—

No single heart
can beat alone;
each one receives
and passes on
the pulse of Family.

Overview

Tracing one's family tree is a popular activity—for good reason. Having an awareness of our ancestors, warts and all, can help us better understand who we are. In addition to our birth families, we can discover another family—a spiritual one. Just as tracing one's biological family tree can prove to be a blessing, the same is true of tracing one's spiritual family tree.

This quiet space encourages participants to look back to the beginning of their conscious awareness of God and to trace the line of those who helped guide them in their spiritual life. Beginning with the first person, place, or event to make a spiritual impression on them and continuing to the present, participants are invited to trace their own spiritual family tree. Participants can pray for each of these individuals and give thanks to God for each person or event that has helped to shape their faith.

Since not all spiritual impressions are positive, the guide gives participants an opportunity to acknowledge even the unpleasant experiences. Naming these negative experiences and praying for those involved in them can be a way of offering them to divine Love for healing.

Developing the Quiet Space

Please read "General Considerations," starting on page 92, before you begin.

ESSENTIALS

- A small area, indoors or outdoors

- A chair or bench and small writing table (or other surface for writing)

- Good lighting

- "Spiritual Family Tree" (page 86) templates—one for each participant

- A completed sample of a Spiritual Family Tree

- Pencils and erasers

- Participant's Guide

- Sign to identify the quiet space: Spiritual Family Tree

OTHER POSSIBILITIES

- A beanbag lap desk in place of a writing table

- A focus area with Bible, cross, icon

- Small trash basket

PROCEDURE

- Arrange space attractively.

- Make enough copies of tree template for each participant to have one.

- Complete one Spiritual Family Tree template and display it as a sample.

- If using a focus area, choose and arrange items.

- Prepare selections from "Appropriate Readings" to place in the space.

- Copy Participant's Guide or adapt it to fit your needs.

- Post sign(s).

- Pray a blessing on this space and on all who come to it.

APPROPRIATE READINGS

- This book open to pages 82–83

- Genesis 2:18

- Psalm 68:6

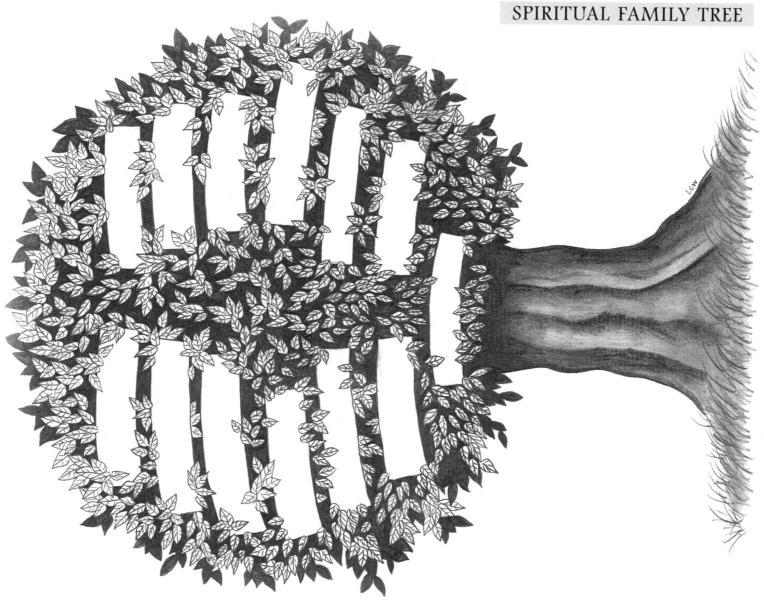

Art by Laurette Clark Wolfe used by permission.
Contemplative by Design © 2008 Gerrie L. Grimsley and Jane J. Young. All rights reserved.

Participant's Guide: SPIRITUAL FAMILY TREE

*T*here is a growing fascination with researching family histories. Whether it stems from a need for genetic information, the goal of locating a family member, or a desire to learn the stories of ancestors' lives, the interest impels people to learn about those who played a role in shaping who they are.

Who has shaped you *spiritually*? If you were to create your spiritual family tree, who would be included in it?

You are invited to:

Look at the sample of a spiritual family tree, then get a blank template and pencil, so you can complete your own.

First, make a list of those persons who have most influenced your inner development. Remember that sometimes it is through our disappointment, pain, or sorrow that we grow spiritually. Naming these negative experiences and praying for those involved in them could be a way of offering them to the divine Love for healing.

With each entry you make in your spiritual family tree, spend time praying for the person you have listed. Give thanks for those who have had a positive influence on you, and pray for growing understanding of those whose influence has seemed negative.

Ask yourself, *Who would list my name on their spiritual family tree?*

Contemplate this question and ask God to show you how to be a spiritual friend or mentor to someone else.

Take your spiritual family tree with you when you leave.

CHAPTER 15

Water

Happy are those who do not follow the advice of the wicked, . . .
but their delight is in the law of the LORD. . . .
They are like trees planted by streams of water,
which yield their fruit in its season,
and their leaves do not wither.
—Psalm 1:1-3

—⁕—

Water, in eternal flow
from past to future, earth to sky,
you bring me beauty,
cleanse, renew, sustain my life
. . . and I?
I bring you but enduring thanks
awash with firm intent
to honor and respect,
not profane, neglect,
your call to purity.

Overview

As it cycles through glaciers, mountain snows, rivers, seas, and clouds, water sustains life on earth. Coming to us simply as a gift, it satisfies the thirst of plant and beast; and neither can survive without it. Both the life-giving nature of water and our desperate need for it make it a powerful metaphor for God and for our longing for relationship with the Sacred.

Psalm 42:1-2 captures our need: "As a deer longs for flowing streams, so my soul longs for you, O God. My soul thirsts for God, for the living God." Psalm 65:9 expresses something of God's nature: "You visit the earth and water it, . . . the river of God is full of water."

The author of Isaiah shares a vision of the prerequisites of meaningful relationship with the Almighty and then says that those who experience it are both watered and become water for others. "If you remove the yoke from among you, the pointing of the finger, the speaking of evil, if you offer your food to the hungry and satisfy the needs of the afflicted, then . . . you shall be like a watered garden, like a spring of water, whose waters never fail" (Isa. 58:9-11).

The Gospel of John also affirms that such a relationship will result in our becoming conduits of the water: "'Out of the believer's heart shall flow rivers of living water'" (John 7:38).

Throughout the centuries since those verses were written, the church has continued to use water to facilitate human awareness of invisible realities. In the service of baptism, water represents the life-giving nature of God and symbolizes the cleansing power of relationship with the divine.

Those who come to this quiet space are invited to:

- consider the role of water in daily life;

- let water speak to them of the sacred.

Developing the Quiet Space

Please read "General Considerations," starting on page 92, before you begin.

ESSENTIALS

- Outdoor space near moving water (an ocean, waterfall, stream, creek, or river) or an indoor space with one or more fountains

- If using a fountain
  > plastic to protect surface where fountain will sit
  > soft, drapeable fabric to cover the plastic, preferably large enough to "flow" to the floor
  > smooth, water-worn stones to secure the fabric

- A comfortable seat: a bench or chair; a rock, stump, or grassy spot with a natural backrest (a rock face or tree, for example). Consider needs of people with physical challenges.

- This book open to pages 88–89

- Participant's Guide

- Sign(s)

OTHER POSSIBILITIES

- Planters containing a variety of plants can add color to an outdoor setting or bring the beauty of nature indoors

PROCEDURES

- Reserve space, if necessary.

- If outdoors, make sure the area is clean and attractive; if indoors, plan arrangement of space and obtain one or more fountains.

- Copy the Participant's Guide or adapt it to fit your needs. Be sure to laminate for use outdoors.

- Arrange the setting. If placing this book in an indoor space, open it to the correct page or pages. If placing it in an outdoor space, insert a note that indicates page or pages to read—and provide a waterproof container to protect it.

- Post sign(s).

- Pray a blessing on this space and on all who come to it.

Participant's Guide: WATER

With deep respect, turn your attention to the water.

Let the sound of the water enter you and move through you.

You may want to dip your fingers into the water, then touch them to your face or arms.

Ask yourself these questions:

- *How has water served me since I awakened this morning?*

- *How have I related to water on other days, in other seasons, places, activities—recreation, avocation, work?*

- *How have I experienced or witnessed the power of water?*

When you are ready, find a comfortable place to sit. Read the pages marked in *Contemplative by Design*. Then, enter into a period of reflection and receptivity by praying the following prayer:

Thank you, River of Life,
for the blessings borne to me by water. In silence
now, I'll listen to the water's song
to hear what it says to me of you.

As you conclude these reflective moments, ponder the fact that your body is nearly 70 percent water. Consider what this means for you and all other living things.

Envision the water cycle and all the animals and plants that drink from this mystic river. What does this reality say of your relationship to all other life forms?

What does the water cycle say of your relationship to the Source of All?

Be open to any word, sense, feeling, or thought that comes to you.

When you leave this place, remember the sounds of the water and your experience here.

Please return this guide to the place where you found it.

General Considerations Applicable to All Quiet Spaces

1. Space

The location of a quiet space will influence its effectiveness. Think through your options.

- Some quiet spaces are designed for outdoors; a few can work well in an open but covered structure, such as a gazebo, picnic shelter, or porch.

- Most quiet spaces will benefit from enclosure, especially if the space is to be used for more than one day. The ideal indoor setting is usually a small room.

- A portion of a large indoor space can serve well if boundaries are clearly indicated:

  a) If the larger area is unattractive or will be in use for other activities, surround the quiet space with room dividers or decorative screens; to soften the effect, drape them with fabric.

  b) If the larger space is attractive and won't be otherwise used, arrange furniture or plants to create quiet space boundaries.

2. Essentials

In each chapter, under the heading "Essentials," the basic supplies, equipment, and furnishings for one quiet space are listed.

3. Other Possibilities

To move beyond the basics, visit the space you plan to use. Stand in it, walk around in it, sit in it, sense what you want it to be and say to those who come. Then, think how to give your vision structure. Note on paper all ideas that come. You may also want to consider the following:

- A copy of this book, open to the appropriate chapter title page and overview, can serve as a helpful introduction to the space.

- In addition to scripture, excerpts from classic or modern literature, plays, poetry, or songs can enrich the experience of those who come. Look for meaningful passages in whatever you read; listen for them wherever you go; look for them in books of quotations; find them online.

- Furniture arrangement will affect appearance, traffic flow, and comfort. Plan carefully. Should some furniture be removed? added?

- Tablecloths or fabric of interesting designs or textures will enhance surfaces on which you will place the quiet space materials. Inventive use of fabric can also improve the appearance of a wall or piece of furniture.

- Pillows, cushions, art, lamps, plants, or flowers can be used in many ways to transform a space.

- Music can block out distracting sounds and add to the ambiance. If you intend to use background music:

    a) Carefully test all equipment before use.

    b) Set the equipment to repeat the musical selection—or leave instructions for how to reset the music for the next user.

    c) If using battery-operated equipment, provide replacement batteries.

    d) Choose music that fits the focus of the quiet space. Instrumental music is preferable to vocal music. Some possibilities:

- Erik Berglund, *Angelic Harp Music*, Oreade Music, 2000

- Zamfir, *The Lonely Shepherd*, Philips, 1990

- Dan Gibson's Solitudes Series, some of which are listed in note 13, page 107.

4. Readings

- All chapters incorporate scripture; some include readings from additional sources. You may want to add other selections.

- Either write out scripture or provide a Bible and a list of scripture references.

- Prepare all readings, even lists of scriptures, so that they're attractive and will resist creases and soil through multiple uses. Consider the following suggestions:

> Write the readings in calligraphy or type them in a large, bold font to make copy more attractive and easier to read.

> Write on, or mount computer-produced copies onto, pieces of colored poster board or construction paper.

> Protect readings by laminating them or covering them with clear contact paper (available where shelf paper is sold).

> Attach strips of folded poster board to back of selections you want to stand upright. (See back of a freestanding picture frame for a guide to shaping the support.)

5. Participant's Guide

Each chapter's sample guide may be copied or adapted for use in the quiet space. If you adapt the guide, make sure it is easy to read, simple to follow, worded exactly for your circumstances.

- Mount the copy on colored poster board or construction paper.

- To keep the guide clean for repeated use, laminate or cover it with clear contact paper.

- If the guide is to be hung (perhaps on an outdoor bench), staple or glue a loop of twine or rope to its back, near the top.

- If you want the guide to stand up on a table, provide an easel, or fold and attach a piece of poster board to the guide's back. (See back of a freestanding picture frame for a guide to shaping the support.)

- If the guide is to be used outside, a plastic box with easy-to-open lid or a waterproof zip-lock bag can offer additional protection.

6. Signs

Readily visible and easy-to-read signs are essential.

- Provide an attractive sign naming each space.

- Another sign reading *"Shh. You're entering a quiet space."* can designate the space and remind passers-by of the need for silence.

- If the quiet space is difficult to locate, provide directional signs along the way.

- If interruptions are a concern, create an "In use" sign. See "Deepening Silence" for one idea.

- If needed, provide stakes on which to mount or hang outdoor signs. Use approved methods for hanging indoor signs; get permission before using tacks or sticky substances on walls or doors.

7. Prayer

Pray spontaneously or use this prayer for blessing each space and all who will come to it:

Life-changing God, I pray that your Spirit, far greater than any human thought or plan, will fill this space. And may it touch with tongue of fire or gentle dove each soul that enters here. Amen.

Suggestions for Further Reading

Allen, Paul M., and Joan D. Allen. *Francis of Assisi's Canticle of the Creatures: A Modern Spiritual Path.* New York: Continuum International, 2000.

Bourgeault, Cynthia. *Centering Prayer and Inner Awakening.* Cambridge, MA.: Cowley Publications, 2004.

Buechner, Frederick. *Listening to Your Life.* San Francisco: HarperSanFrancisco, 1992.

Davey, H. E. *Brush Meditation: A Japanese Way to Mind and Body Harmony.* Berkeley, CA: Stone Bridge Press, 1999.

Doughty, Steve. *To Walk in Integrity.* Nashville, TN: Upper Room Books, 2006.

Dunnam, Maxie. *Workbook of Intercessory Prayer.* Nashville, TN: Upper Room Books, 1997.

Foster, Richard J. *Freedom of Simplicity.* San Francisco: HarperSanFrancisco, 1981.

Ganim, Barbara, and Susan Fox. *Visual Journaling: Going Deeper than Words.* Wheaton, IL: Quest Books, Theosophical Publishing House, 1999.

Harper, Steve. *Talking in the Dark: Praying When Life Doesn't Make Sense.* Nashville, TN: Upper Room Books, 2007.

Helminski, Kabir Edmund. *Living Presence: A Sufi Way to Mindfulness and the Essential Self.* New York: Jeremy P. Tarcher/Putnam Penguin, 1992.

Keating, Thomas, M. Basil Pennington, and Thomas Clarke. *Finding Grace at the Center.* Petersham, MA.: Saint Bede's Publications, 1978.

Kincannon, Karla M. *Creativity and Divine Surprise: Finding the Place of Your Resurrection.* Nashville, TN: Upper Room Books, 2005.

May, Gerald G. *The Dark Night of the Soul: A Psychiatrist Explores the Connection between Darkness and Spiritual Growth.* San Francisco: HarperSanFrancisco, 2004.

Miller, Wendy J. *Invitation to Presence.* Nashville, TN: Upper Room Books, 1993.

Morgan, Richard L. *Remembering Your Story: Creating Your Own Spiritual Autobiography,* rev. ed. Nashville, TN: Upper Room Books, 2002.

Morris, Robert Corin. *Provocative Grace: The Challenge in Jesus' Words.* Nashville, TN: Upper Room Books, 2006.

Mulholland, M. Robert, Jr. *Shaped by the Word: The Power of Scripture in Spiritual Formation.* Rev. ed. Nashville, TN: Upper Room Books, 2002.

Nouwen, Henri J. M. *Can You Drink the Cup?* Notre Dame, IN: Ave Maria Press, 1996.

———. *Bread for the Journey: A Daybook of Wisdom and Faith.* San Francisco: HarperSanFrancisco, 1997.

Norberg, Tilda, and Robert D. Webber. *Stretch Out Your Hand: Exploring Healing Prayer.* Nashville, TN: Upper Room Books, 1999.

Redding, Mary Lou. *The Power of a Focused Heart: 8 Life Lessons from the Beatitudes.* Nashville, TN: Upper Room Books, 2006.

Stroble, Paul E. *You Gave Me a Wide Place: Holy Places of Our Lives.* Nashville, TN: Upper Room Books, 2006.

Thompson, Marjorie J. *Soul Feast: An Invitation to the Christian Spiritual Life.* Louisville, KY: Westminster John Knox Press, 1995.

Wilson, Patricia. *Quiet Spaces: Prayer Interludes for Women.* Nashville, TN: Upper Room Books, 2002.

Wuellner, Flora Slosson. *Feed My Shepherds: Spiritual Healing and Renewal for Those in Christian Leadership.* Nashville, TN: Upper Room Books, 1998.

Vennard, Jane E., and Stephen D. Bryant. *The Way of Prayer, Participant's Book.* Companions in Christ. Nashville, TN: Upper Room Books, 2007.

Appendixes

APPENDIX 1

Optional Plan for the Art quiet space: If you prefer that participants create art instead of, or in addition to, viewing art, consider the following.

Developing the Quiet Space: Art

Please read "General Considerations," starting on page 92, before you begin.

ESSENTIALS

- A space appropriate for the chosen creative process

- Readings from scripture and other sources

- Two chairs or benches, one to place near reading materials, one to place at art supplies

- Supplies for the creative activity

- Surface on which to place scriptures and other readings

- Surface(s) on which to place art supplies and on which to complete the creative activity

- Participant's Guide

- Sign designating the quiet space: "Art"

PROCEDURE

- Choose and reserve space.

- Provide a surface on which participants may place their completed work—perhaps in a simple worship setting.

- Select and prepare scripture and other readings. See chapter 2, page 19 for readings.

- Choose a medium for participants to use: paint, clay, tiles, a variety of materials. That decision made, note supplies and equipment needed and develop instructions to include on the Participant's Guide. For example, if you choose paint, supplies and equipment will include paints, brushes, small canvases or art paper, an easel or flat surface on which to work, water in which to clean brushes, handi-wipes for cleanup, a trash can, a surface on which to place completed paintings. Instructions on the Participant's Guide might include the following:

a) Sit quietly for several minutes, eyes closed. Instead of picturing a painting you would like to create, sense your inner feelings and what you feel from the space around you.

b) Become aware of colors you associate with these feelings.

c) When ready, open your eyes, dip brushes into colors, and let the colors "choose" where they want to go on the canvas or paper. (This process is based on an exercise by Karla Kincannon.)

If you choose clay, you will need lumps of clay, an attractive container to hold them, handi-wipes for cleanup, a trash can, a surface on which to place finished products—perhaps in a simple worship setting. Instructions on the Participant's Guide might include:

a) Sit quietly for a few minutes, then take a lump of clay and work with it for a while with a sense of waiting, of receptivity, simply becoming comfortable with the feel of the substance in your hands.

b) Consider what a lump of clay and a human life have in common.

c) Contemplate your relationship with your Creator—what it is, what it may become.

d) When ready, shape a symbol: something that represents who you see yourself to be at this time, something that represents your current relationship with God, or something that represents a significant yearning so far as that relationship is concerned.

If you choose for participants to work with several materials, your supplies might include backing, adhesive, scissors, pebbles, tiles, lengths of colored yarn, buttons, scraps of fabric, and, if only adults will be involved, pieces of broken mirror, glass, pottery. (Small artist's tiles, pebbles, adhesive, and so forth are available at craft stores.) Instructions on the Participant's Guide may include:

a) Contemplate aspects of your life that are light, dark, soft, hard, flowing, tangled, open, closed.

b) Consider how those aspects of your life are parts of the whole—which dominate, which play minor roles, which flow through you in other ways. Are you aware of some that always influence the others? Do some only occasionally exert dramatic influence?

c) Create a piece to express these perceptions.

- Prepare the Participant's Guide: Into the Guide provided, insert your own instructions or instructions you choose from those listed above.

- Gather all supplies and equipment.

- Arrange the setting.

- Post sign(s).

- Pray a blessing on this space and on all who come to it.

Participant's Guide: CREATION OF ART

Take a seat and read from the scriptures and quotes from other sources.

Spend time quietly considering the creative force that brought the world into being and continues to work in each of us.

Move to the art supplies. Acknowledge the Creator. Offer your open hands.

[Insert appropriate instructions for working with the materials provided.]

When you have finished, look at your work carefully to see if it reveals something you did not realize was there.

In prayer, offer whatever your art represents to you.

Place the piece on the surface provided or, if you prefer, take it with you as a reminder of your experience in this quiet space.

Use handi-wipes for cleanup.

Return this guide and all supplies to their original locations.

APPENDIX 2

Suggestions for guided responses if viewing tapestry, mosaic, or mixed-media art for chapter 2, "Art."

If using a tapestry:

- Choose a scrap of fabric to hold while viewing the art.

- Consider how texture and color are part of the beauty of the tapestry and, in different ways, the scrap of fabric.

- Contemplate what produces darker and brighter shades and differing textures in life.

- Ponder the effect of relationship with God on the beauty and texture of a life being woven from daily attitudes, perceptions, and experiences.

If using a mosaic or a mixed-media piece that includes tiles, pebbles, for example:

- Look at the art meditatively.

- Take a tile (or pebble, or any material used in that art that you've supplied) and hold it while viewing the work.

- Pay attention to the feel of it.

- Contemplate its use in the work of art: What role does it play?

- Consider what it might symbolize in the development of your life. Might it represent something hard or challenging that can ultimately add texture, color, and beauty to the you that you are co-creating? Is there a different perspective from which you might look at your circumstances in order to see them differently or position them differently within the whole of your life?

- How do your perceptions of God and your relationship with God affect who you are becoming?

APPENDIX 3
Guided Meditation Script
for chapter 3, "Believing Power"

If you choose to record the Participant's Guide for the Believing Power quiet space, you will need: (1) recording equipment capable of producing good quality sound; (2) a sturdy and simple-to-use CD player; (3) a reader with a strong, pleasant voice, and (4) plenty of batteries or a convenient outlet into which to plug your player.

SCRIPT
Now hear the story of Jesus and the woman with the issue of blood as read from Matthew's Gospel, chapter 9, verses 20 to 22:

> Just then a woman who had been subject to bleeding for twelve years came up behind him and touched the edge of his cloak. She said to herself, "If I only touch his cloak, I will be healed." Jesus turned and saw her. "Take heart, daughter," he said, "your faith has healed you." And that woman was healed from that moment.

Consider a need you have for healing in your life. Or perhaps consider the need of someone who is on your heart right now.

[PAUSE 15 SECONDS]

Choose a rolled piece of cloth from the container, unroll it, and lay it over your lap.

[PAUSE 15 SECONDS]

Sitting in a comfortable position, with the cloth you have chosen on your lap, slowly inhale deeply. Slowly exhale. [PAUSE 10 SECONDS]

Listen to the story being read a second time. This time see yourself or your friend in need in the crowd. [READ A BIT MORE SLOWLY THIS TIME.]

> Just then a woman who had been subject to bleeding for twelve years came up behind him and touched the edge of his cloak. She said to herself, "If I only touch his cloak, I will be healed." Jesus turned and saw her. "Take heart, daughter," he said, "your faith has healed you." And that woman was healed from that moment.

Now replay the scene in your mind's eye. Try to:
> - hear the sounds [PAUSE 10 SECONDS];
> - feel the heat of the day [PAUSE 10 SECONDS];
> - sense the excitement of the people hoping to

get a glimpse of Jesus [PAUSE 10 SECONDS];

> taste the dust rising up from the street [PAUSE 10 SECONDS];

Take in the smells . . . [PAUSE 10 SECONDS]

> the heavy salt-filled air from the sea,
> food being cooked by street vendors,
> bodies pressing in from the crowd.

[PAUSE 10 SECONDS]

Notice the twelve men walking protectively beside, behind, and in front of Jesus as they try to hurry him on his way. [PAUSE 10 SECONDS]

Now put yourself in the place of the woman. Become the person who seeks Jesus. You are timid, with good reason; your head is cast down and almost completely covered.

Watch as the villagers quickly move away to avoid contact with you. Hear the murmurs getting louder with each step you take into the crowd. Feel your struggle between hesitancy and determination. Feel the desperate need. You've heard many stories about this Jesus who can heal and cast out demons. You have dreamed of this moment.

Reflect on several questions:

[PAUSE 10 SECONDS AFTER EACH QUESTION.]

What am I thinking?

What am I feeling?

What is my hesitancy? How am I weighing my struggle?

What has finally determined my decision to take this frightening step of faith?

Now leave the story for a while and recall the need you named earlier. As you feel ready, respond to the following questions:

[PAUSE 10–20 SECONDS AFTER EACH ONE.]

What needs to be healed in me or my friend?

Is the need for physical healing? relational? emotional? spiritual?

Does the need stem from an attitude, such as prejudice? fear? resentment? fatigue? confusion? addiction? unbelief? anger? painful memories? unforgiving spirit?

Stay with your need for a while. [PAUSE 10 SECONDS.] Here are some other questions to consider:

[PAUSE 10 SECONDS AFTER EACH QUESTION.]

How has this need affected my life?

How has it affected the lives of others?

How long have I lived with it?

Am I sure I want to give it up?

Am I willing to trust the Healer with this issue?

Do I trust—

in God's perfect timing?

the method God chooses for healing?

that whatever I go through to realize healing ultimately will be in my best interest?

Take any concern you may have to God now, knowing that God has already heard your heart's words. If you doubt, ask God to take whatever little bit of faith you have and hold it under the light of divine power and grace. If you are afraid, ask for God's strength to take one step at a time.

[PAUSE 15 SECONDS.]

When you are ready, think back again to the story. Focus on the woman with the issue of blood as she finds the strength to reach out in faith and touch Jesus' cloak.

[PAUSE 15 SECONDS.]

Now pick up the cloth you placed on your lap. allow it to be for you a symbol of Christ's cloak. There is no magic in this cloth, and it is by no means sacred, but use it to connect your life with the life of the woman in need and as a way of saying, *I, too, am willing to take this step, to reach out to Jesus, my Healer.*

Place the cloth over an area of your body that symbolizes the location of your pain or brokenness. For example, if you need healing of a way of thinking or perceiving, you may want to cover your head with the cloth. Or, if your need is more relational or emotional, you could hold the cloth close to your heart.

[PAUSE 15 SECONDS.]

Once again, in your mind's eye, return to the story and watch as Jesus turns around and sees that it is you who touched his cloak this time.

[PAUSE 30 SECONDS.]

Hear the authority and kindness in his voice as he says to you, "Take heart, my child, your faith has healed you."

[PAUSE 10 SECONDS.]

Stay for a moment and soak in these words of Jesus. Respond to him in any way you choose.

[PAUSE 30 SECONDS.]

When you are ready to leave this quiet space, take your piece of cloth with you as a reminder that the Healer has heard your cry, knows your need. God longs to heal you in God's perfect timing and way. As you leave, go in peace. Go, believing in God's power.

Please turn off the CD player before you leave.

Notes

Introduction

1. George Appleton, *Journey for a Soul* (Glasgow: William Collins Sons & Co. / Fontana Books, 1974), 38.

Chapter 1: All of Life

1. C. S. Lewis, *Letters to Malcolm: Chiefly on Prayer* (San Diego: Harcourt Brace Jovanovich Publishers, 1964), 75.

Chapter 2: Art

1. Sylvia Everett, artist-in-residence at Andover Newton Theological School, 1995–2001, in an e-mail to Jane Young, 2007.
2. Jan Steward and Corita Kent, *Learning by Heart: Teaching to Free the Creative Spirit* (New York: Bantam Books, 1992), 4–5.
3. Gertrud Mueller Nelson, *To Dance with God: Family Ritual and Community Celebration* (New York/Mahwah, NJ: Paulist Press, 1986), 42.
4. Deena Metzger, *Writing for Your Life: A Guide and Companion to the Inner Worlds* (San Francisco: HarperSanFrancisco, 1992), 193.
5. Clarissa Pinkola Estés, *Women Who Run with the Wolves: Myths and Stories of the Wild Woman Archetype* (New York: Ballantine Books, 1992), 298.

Chapter 3: Believing Power

1. Steve Harper, *Talking in the Dark: Praying When Life Doesn't Make Sense* (Nashville, TN: Upper Room Books, 2007), 53.
2. C. S. Lewis, *A Grief Observed* (New York: Bantam Books, 1976), 25.
3. Harper, *Talking in the Dark*, 15.

Chapter 4: Bread and Juice

1. Henri J. M. Nouwen, *Can You Drink the Cup?* (Notre Dame, IN: Ave Maria Press, 1996), 19–21.

Chapter 5: Breath, Wind, Spirit

1. Paul J. Achtemeierr, ed., *Harper's Bible Dictionary* (New York: Harper and Row, 1985), 401.

Chapter 8: Flame and Dance

1. *Merriam-Webster's Collegiate Dictionary*, 11th ed., s.v. "spirit."

2. For pottery oil lamps designed to remain lit when held by dancers, and to burn dependably, contact June Keener Wink at Wild Thyme Pottery, Sandisfield, MA 01255, tel. 413-258-4243, or jkwthyme@bcn.net. These lamps also have broad bases that prevent tipping.

3. Ann Weems, *Reaching for Rainbows: Resources for Creative Worship* (Philadelphia, PA: Westminster Press, 1980), 61–62.

4. Metzger, *Writing for Your Life*, 197.

5. Weems, *Reaching for Rainbows*, 91–92.

Chapter 9: God's Rest

1. Lewis Carroll, *Through the Looking-glass and What Alice Found There* (New York: William Morrow and Co., 1993), 42.

2. A. J. Russell, ed., *God Calling* (Uhrichsville, OH: Barbour Publishing, 1998), February 16.

Chapter 12: Love's Sacrifice

1. John Mogabgab, in conversation with Gerrie Grimsley. John is editor of *Weavings: A Journal of the Christian Spiritual Life*. www.weavings.org

Chapter 13: Nature

1. CDs with music featuring nature sounds include these three by Dan Gibson, from Solitudes:

Celtic Awakening, 1997
Mountain Sunrise: Peaceful Pan Flutes, 1999
Pachelbel: In the Garden, 2003

2. Metzger, *Writing for Your Life*, 214.

3. Fyodor Dostoyevsky, *The Brothers Karamazov*, trans. Constance Garnett (New York: Modern Library / Random House [1950]), 382–83.

Photo Credits

Chapter 2, page 16: Mosaic by Sylvia Everett, former artist-in-residence, Andover Newton Theological School. Her mosaics, tapestries, painting, free-form embroideries, and mixed-media pieces may be seen online at www.WisdomsTable.net. Photo by James T. Pennell.

Chapter 9, page 58: Photo by James H. Johnson, Hermitage, Tennessee.

Chapter 12, page 72: Art by anonymous artist, Uganda. Photo by Greg Grimsley.

Chapter 13, page 76: Photo by Greg Grimsley, Sr.

Chapter 15, page 88: Source of the Nile. Photo by Gerrie Grimsley.

About the Authors

JANE J. YOUNG is a retired teacher. Her interests include dancing with a liturgical dance group, writing, spending time with family, and singing with Womansong, a performance choral group based in Asheville, NC. Previously published works include several poems and a book, *Settling Estates in North Carolina: A Step-by-Step Guide.* She and her husband, Garland, live at Lake Junaluska, North Carolina.

GERRIE L. GRIMSLEY serves as assistant to the director of Pathways in Congregational Spirituality at Upper Room Ministries. She has led mission trips to India, Uganda, and Zimbabwe. Gerrie enjoys writing, creative picture books for children, and doting on her grandchildren. Previously published works include meditations and poems. She lives near Nashville, Tennessee, with her husband, Greg.

Other Titles of Interest

The Retreat Leader's Manual:
A Complete Guide to Organizing Meaningful
Christian Retreats
Nancy Ferguson and Kevin Witt
ISBN 0-88177-428-6

Retreats for Renewal:
5 Models for Intergenerational Weekends
Nancy Ferguson
ISBN 978-0-88177-515-0

Creativity and Divine Surprise:
Finding the Place of Your Resurrection
Karla Kincannon
ISBN 0-8358-9812-1

Openings:
A Daybook of Saints, Psalms, and Prayer
Larry James Peacock
ISBN 0-8358-9850-4

You Gave Me a Wide Place:
Holy Places of Our Lives
Paul E. Stroble
ISBN 0-8358-1002-X

Journeying Through the Days:
A Calendar & Journal for Personal Reflection
an illustrated annual publication

The Upper Room Disciplines: A Book of Daily Devotions
a multiauthor annual publication

Find at your local bookstore
Call 1-800-972-0433
or
Order online at www.UpperRoom.org/bookstore